DISCARDED

THE CHICKAMAUGA CAMPAIGN

Ohio troops storm a Rebel battery at the Battle of Stones River.

Pontoon bridge lies in front of railroad bridge destroyed by Bragg's army to hinder pursuit by Union forces as Bragg retreated through Tennessee.

★The Great Military Campaigns of History★

THE
CHICKAMAUGA CAMPAIGN

December 1862–November 1863

Patrick Abbazia

GALLERY BOOKS
An imprint of W.H. Smith Publishers Inc.
112 Madison Avenue
New York, New York 10016

For the Treasure, Linguini, and the Little Bear—
they know why

Prepared by Combined Books
26 Summit Grove, Suite 207
Bryn Mawr, PA 19010

Project Director: Robert L. Pigeon
Project Coordinator: Antoinette Bauer
Editor of the Series: Albert A. Nofi
Photographic Research: John Cannan
Layout: Kirsten Kerr
Maps: Kevin Wilkins

Produced by Wieser and Wieser, Inc.
118 East 25th Street, New York, NY 10010

This 1988 edition published by Gallery Books, an
imprint of
W.H. Smith Publishers, Inc., 112 Madison Avenue,
New York, NY 10016.

Library of Congress Cataloging-in-Publication Data

Abbazia, Patrick.
    The Chickamauga campaign, December 1862-November 1863.

    Bibliography: p. 183
    1. Chickamauga, Battle of, 1863.   2. Tennessee—
History—Civil War, 1861-1865—Campaigns.
I. Title.
E475.81.A22 1988   973.7'35   88-5067
ISBN 0-8317-1257-0

CONTENTS

Federal mounted infantry patrols the Nashville and Chattanooga railroad to prevent sabotage by Confederates.

MAPS

Cumberland Heights.

★The Great Military Campaigns of History★

PREFACE TO THE SERIES

Jonathan Swift termed war "that mad game the world so loves to play". He had a point. Universally condemned, it has nevertheless been almost as universally practiced. For good or ill, war has played a significant role in the shaping of history. Indeed, there is hardly a human institution which has not in some fashion been influenced and molded by war, even as it helped shape and mold war in turn. Yet the study of war has been as remarkably neglected as its practice has been commonplace. With a few outstanding exceptions, the history of wars and of military operations has until quite recently been largely the province of the inspired patriot or the regimental polemicist. Only in our times have serious, detailed, and objective accounts come to be considered the norm in the treatment of military history and related matters. Yet there still remains a gap in the literature, for there are two types of military history. One type is written from a very serious, highly technical, professional perspective and presupposes that the reader is deeply familiar with background, technology, and general situation. The other is perhaps less dry, but merely lightly reviews the events with the intention of informing and entertaining the layman. The qualitative gap between the two is vast. Moreover, there are professionals in both the military and in academia whose credentials are limited to particular moments in the long, sad history of war, and there are laymen who have a more than passing understanding of the field; and then there is the concerned citizen, interested in understanding the phenomenon in an age of unusual violence and unprecedented armaments. It is to bridge the gap between the two types of military history, and to reach the professional and the serious amateur and the concerned citizen alike, that this series, *The Great Campaigns of Military History,* is designed.

The individual volumes of *The Great Campaigns of Military History* are each devoted to an intensive examination of a particularly significant military operation. The focus is not on individual battles, but on campaigns, on the relationship between movements and battles and how they fit within the overall framework of the war in question. By making use of a series of innovative techniques for the presentation of information, *The Great Campaigns of Military History* can satisfy the exacting demands of the professional and the serious amateur, while making it possible for the concerned citizen to understand the events and the conditions under which they developed. This is accomplished in a number of ways. Each volume contains a substantial, straight-forward narrative account of the campaign under study. This is supported by an extensive series of modular "sidebars". Some are devoted to particular specific technical matters, such as weaponry, logistics, organization, or tactics. These modules each contain detailed analyses of their topic, and make considerable use of "hard" data, with many charts and tables. Other modules deal with less technical matters, such as strategic analysis, anecdotes, personalities, uniforms, and politics. Each volume contains several detailed maps, supplemented by a number of clear, accurate sketchmaps, which assist the reader in understanding the course of events under consideration, and there is an extensive set of illustrations which have been selected to assist the reader still further. Finally, each volume contains materials designed to help the reader who is interested in learning more. But this "bibliography" includes not merely a short list of books and articles related to the campaign in question. It also contains information on study groups devoted to the subject, on films which deal with it, on recordings of period music, on simulation games and skirmish clubs which attempt to recreate the tactics, on museums where one can have a first-hand look at equipment, and on tours of the battlefields. The particular contents of each volume will, of course, be determined by the topic in question, but each will provide an unusually rich and varied treatment of the subject. Each volume in *The Great Campaigns of Military History* is thus not merely an account of a particular military operation, but it is a unique reference to the theory and practice of war in the period in question.

The Great Campaigns of Military History is a unique contribution to the study of war and of military history, which will remain of interest and use for many years.

Albert A. Nofi
Editor-in-Chief

Stevenson, Alabama, the supply base of the Army of the Cumberland.

INTRODUCTION

It was deep into the dark night of Saturday, 19 September 1863, and it was unusually cool for that time of year in the woodlands along Chickamauga Creek, near the Tennessee-Georgia line. The smoky woods smelled of the random fires and acrid clouds of gunpowder caused by the day's fierce, bloody battle. In clearings all about that wild, gloomy forest landscape, chilled, exhausted soldiers forced tasteless rations into dry mouths, listlessly cleaned their rifles, or wandered erratically through the dark. They searched out missing friends, helped carry in bloody, mangled wounded men, or simply sat huddled against the frosty air and the dread of the morrow. Some of them were close enough to the hospital tents to hear the grinding-singing-rasping of the surgeons' saws shearing through human bone and the piercing screams of smashed, hurting men. Although they could not know it in the dark, the nearby pond was stained red with the blood of the parched wounded who dragged themselves there to drink. Such was the end of the first long day of the Battle of Chickamauga.

One of the troubled, restless men on that fearful night was a brand-new Confederate lieutenant general. His name was D. H. Hill, and he commanded a corps in General Braxton Bragg's Army of Tennessee. Harvey Hill was an aggressive, irascible, confident South Carolinian; at once cocky and touchy, he was, like many of the South's best combat leaders, a welcome friend on the battlefield and a difficult companion in the barracks. But now dashing Harvey Hill was a quiet, worried man, trapped in a stalemated battle, with deep foreboding of the morrow. Yet this was so unlike him—so much so that he did not understand all of the reasons for his gloom. Moodily, he sensed that his fears were not primarily a product of reason, but were born more of instinct, of feeling. Harvey Hill

knew that there was something deeply wrong, desperately flawed, in the Army of Tennessee. He was not exactly sure what this wrong thing was, or what caused it, but he knew it was there, and it was getting worse, spreading, slowly corroding the will of this army—he was sure of it; there were too many clues to ignore.

Perhaps Harvey Hill was best able to sense the secret, fatal flaw of the Army of Tennessee because he was so new to it, and could examine it with an outsider's perspective. He had been with the army only a matter of days, not weeks. He had arrived in good fettle, happy at his promotion, and not displeased as many would be to serve again with Braxton Bragg; as a young officer in the Mexican War he had served in Bragg's battery of field artillery, and he realized that if Bragg was cold, and strict, and petty, and quarrelsome, he was at least also energetic and efficient. Hill anticipated no difficulty in serving anew under his old chief.

Braxton Bragg had a long, narrow face, large ears, and sad eyes that looked out from deep hollows under big, bushy brows; he had a large, but neatly kept, gray-flecked beard and mustache. He had not aged badly, but when Harvey Hill first saw Bragg again in that fateful September of 1863, he was shocked. Bragg looked unspeakably worn, somehow shrunken in soul, dispirited. Hill found him "silent and . . . gloomy and despondent. He had grown prematurely old . . . and showed much nervousness." Bragg was withdrawn and shaky.

If Bragg seemed to be losing confidence in himself, Hill also realized that the army was at the same time also losing confidence in him. Hill understood that the stern and vindictive strain in Bragg's personality acted as a corrosive upon the proud, touchy men he led and helped create many bitter feuds and rifts that impeded the smooth functioning of the army and caused

Daniel Harvey Hill.

Blundering Braxton Bragg, commander of the Army of Tennessee. Possibly the worst general of the Confederacy, he was unloved by his men and loathed by his lieutenants. A personal friendship with Jefferson Davis was one of the primary reasons why he was able to keep a combat command for so long.

men to doubt their leader's judgment and ability.

But, to Hill, Bragg's main problem was that he was unlucky. He did not win battles. As Hill said, Bragg's "retreats . . . had taken away that enthusiasm which soldiers feel for a successful general, and which makes them obey his orders without question. . . . The one thing that a soldier never fails to understand is victory. . . ."

If Bragg was down, Hill soon found, so was the army. This Western army had a futile, hangdog quality about it that surprised and depressed Hill. He came from the East. He was used to the easy, jaunty, superb confidence of the Army of Northern Virginia. Those soldiers expected, knew even, that they would beat the Yankees whenever and wherever they met them. This army, these soldiers, did not have

that feeling and belief. This army would fight, and even fight hard and well, for its leaders were proud and gallant and its troops were tough and dogged; but it would fight the way the Yankee army in the East, the *Army of the Potomac*, fought, grimly and bravely, but all the while knowing that it could not win.

The Army of Tennessee would fight hard at Chickamauga. But it knew it would not win.

In order to understand how this came to be, it is necessary to move back in time almost a year and in space in a northwesterly direction to the vicinity of Nashville—to go all the way back to the outset of the great battle for the state and river called Tennessee—to understand the causes of the ultimate destruction of the army which also bore that same name.

CHAPTER I

THE CIVIL WAR IN CENTRAL TENNESSEE, 1862

By the fall of 1862, Union armies were fitfully assailing the Confederacy at three key points along a wide arc that stretched 2,000 miles from the coasts of Virginia to the mouth of the Mississippi. In the East, the *Army of the Potomac*, under a succession of mediocre commanders, fought hard, doomed battles north of Richmond against the main Confederate field army, the Army of Northern Virginia, led by the redoubtable R. E. "Bobby" Lee. All the way at the other end of this vast, sprawling front, Union commander U. S. "Sam" Grant's Western army struggled mightily against the Rebs and nature to control the Mississippi River in its entirety. And in the center of this great arc, at Nashville, Tennessee, another strong Union army, under a new leader, prepared to strike southeast toward Chattanooga and the central heartland of the Confederate States of America.

Tennessee was vital to the fortunes of the Civil War. It was the center of the long outer defensive periphery of the Confederacy and the gateway to the vital central heartland of the South, which provided much of the grain and meat, light industry, metals and munitions, and horses and mules which sustained the war effort of the Confederacy, as well as serving as the Hub of the South's east-west-railroad network. Thus, Tennessee was strategically and economically indispensable to the Confederacy because its loss would lead inevitably to disaster in the vital central heartland of the South.

Braxton Bragg's Army of Tennessee lay southeast of Nashville, near Murfreesboro, resting after its invasion, or raid, into Kentucky. In October, at Perryville, southeast of Louisville, Bragg's army had, as it often did, won an indecisive tactical victory over a Union army commanded by portly, lethargic Maj. Gen. Don Carlos Buell, Bragg had hurt part of Buell's army heartily, but the rest was intact, and Bragg's force had been hard hit in return—these early Civil War armies did not possess much tactical finesse, but they could take a lot of killing—and was poised at the perilous tip of an exiguous supply line. It had had to conquer or retreat. Bragg was uncertain if he was strong enough to conquer; so he decided to retreat to Tennessee, where he could readily supply his army. This decision was not popular with the young fire-eaters in the army, particularly the Kentuckians, spurred by resolve to liberate their state.

Bragg, in turn, was not pleased with the performance of his army. His cold, strict ways would not permit him to become reconciled to the vagaries of his individualistic volunteers. He thought them a rabble, brash, contentious, and unreliable. Intense and moody, Bragg was sensitive, but not intellectual. He placed his faith in rules and doctrine, training and regulations, which he saw as solid, firm, eternal. He distrusted ideas; they were rubbery and transient, a poor foundation to support a man's career. So Bragg went by the book; but he was at a loss as to what to do about subordinates and an army that had never read the book. And worse, like many men of few ideas, Bragg clung to the few ideas that he did have with a relentless tenacity. As a man, he was rigid in personality; as a general, he was inflexible in his tactics.

Bragg's earnestness and desire to fit all of the subtleties and complexities of military life into a compact Procrustean bed of strict regulations and a few simple tactical maxims led him into constant quarrels with others. He could not countenance the idea that the rules upon which he ordered his life might be wrong; so Bragg could never be wrong, because his rules and regulations could never be wrong. Accordingly, when events in his command did not go well, he knew that the cause was not in himself—it had to lay in others. So, after Perryville, Braxton

Bragg began to seek scapegoats for his army's repulse in Kentucky. He lashed out at undisciplined volunteers and disloyal subordinates, never understanding that these men had powerful constituencies within not only the army itself, but within the political structures of their home states, and in some cases, friends in the corridors of power in the central government at Richmond. To persist in such potentially divisive internecine vendettas was to put at risk the very cohesion of the army. But Bragg could not stop himself; like many long addicted to a self-destructuve course, he found the ride to destruction exhilerating.

Sam Grant, who knew him in the Old Army, wrote of Bragg: "Bragg was a remarkably intelligent and well-informed man. . . . He was also thoroughly upright. But he was possessed of an irascible temper, and was naturally disputatious. A man of the highest . . . character . . . yet in the old army he was in frequent trouble. As a subordinate he was always on the lookout to catch his commanding officer infringing his prerogatives; as a . . . commander he was equally vigilant to detect the slightest neglect . . . of the most trivial order." His dedication kept him almost constantly at work; and he got too little sleep. His self-generated pressures caused him periodic intense headaches and stomach pain. In the Old Army, an attempt was made to "frag" him; a heavily charged shell was detonated outside his tent, two feet from where he lay asleep. Bragg survived, in a minor sort of miracle; but what is more interesting is his reaction to this miscarried attempt to assassinate him. He was astounded; he said that he did not think that he "had an enemy in the world."

Bragg's incessant preoccupation with rules and ceaseless striving for perfection in small things is best captured by a tale of the Old Army. According to the story, Bragg was serving as chief quartermaster at an army post when the post commander was detached to other duty; Bragg, next in the chain of command, thus became acting post commander. As acting post commander, he submitted a requisition to the chief quartermaster—himself. In his role as chief quartermaster, he rejected and declined to fill the requisition of the acting post commander—also himself. He then sent several letters to and from himself, justifying in turn the point of view of both the acting post commander and the chief quartermaster in the matter of the rejected requisition. Finally, he sent the file on to higher authority for decision. His superior is alleged to have told him: "My God, Mr. Bragg, you have

Don Carlos Buell.

quarreled with every officer in the army, and now you are quarreling with yourself!"

So now the Army of Tennessee waited in the vicinity of Murfreesboro, just starting on the long, bitter process of tearing itself apart—and suddenly it grew weaker. In order to stave off the tenacious Grant along the Mississippi, Bragg was ordered to give up a full division and send it westward. Now, Bragg realized, he would have to go on the defensive in Tennessee; he was not strong enough to attack. Of course, in the East, this numerical technicality never stopped Lee from taking the offensive.

Bragg argued to President Jefferson Davis that the loss of a full division from his army would simply entice the Union army at Nashville to attack him. But Davis, determined to make use of the Confederacy's sole great strategic advantage, that of interior lines, was intent upon trying rapidly to build up a concentration of force strong enough to beat Grant at the most threatened point of the long Confederate perimeter. If Grant was thrown back, then Rebel forces could be shifted quickly northeastward to Tennessee to succor Bragg. But, Bragg wanted to know what would happen if the Yankee army struck hard in Tennessee in the meantime. Davis told him he would have to take a soldier's chance. "Fight if you can," he advised, and if compelled to, "fall back beyond the Tennessee." Bragg knew that he, at the least, had to try to hold on to the dominating high ground overlooking the Tennessee at Chattanooga, gateway to the heartland of the Confederacy.

And so Bragg and his men waited restlessly in Tennessee for their foes to strike.

At Nashville, the Union *Army of the Cumberland* had a new commander. The disjointed encounter battle of Perryville (8 October 1862) had claimed the career of Buell. The question then arose, about who would replace him. The zealous, portly Secretary of War, Edwin McMasters Stanton, wanted one of the army's corps commanders, Maj. Gen. George Henry Thomas, a strapping, laconic old pro from Virginia, to get the job. It is hard to understand why. Stanton, a man with a round, cherubic face, full bushy beard, and little wire-rimmed glasses that seemed even smaller on his large head, had an outward appearance of mildness and calmness, but inside his heart beat wildly with fierce hatred for the Rebels who would destroy his beloved Union in the name of the degraded institution of human slavery. He distrusted Southerners and Democrats alike, and

he detested most of the high professional soldiers who came within his passionate ken. He found them too cool and technical. They did not burn with fury at their foes, the Rebels, most of whose high officers they seemed to know and like; and they were not at all eager to make the war a crusade against slavery. Like most amateurs of the military art, he was concerned primarily with strategy and tactics; but his professional soldiers seemed more concerned with the dismal art of logistics. They always seemed to have ample reasons why a thing could not be done, but were invariably barren of advice as to how to get things done. So it was odd that a man of Stanton's temperament and predilections should sponsor for a post of great responsibility a veteran professional officer who was also a Southerner. Stanton somehow knew that Thomas was a hard-fighting soldier. So he wanted him. Indeed, that was the greatness of Stanton. So strong and inflexible was his passion to destroy the Rebels and all their odious works that he was willing to sacrifice all else— even his own personal prejudices—to the great

Jefferson Davis, president of the Confederate States of America, with his wife. Davis made a major error by maintaining Bragg in a combat command of importance, a mistake which probably cost the South the war.

Braxton Bragg (1817–1876)

Born in North Carolina, Bragg graduated fifth in the West Point class of 1837. He served in the artillery against the Seminoles, on the frontier, and in Mexico, where he particularly distinguished himself (three brevets). He left the Old Army as a lieutenant colonel in 1856, becoming a planter in Louisiana. Appointed a brigadier in Confederate service at the outbreak of the Civil War, Bragg commanded on the Gulf coast in 1861 and was then given a corps in time for Shiloh. A personal friend of Confederate President Jefferson Davis, the latter made Bragg a full general and gave him the Army of Ten-

Braxton Bragg.

nessee in June of 1862. His career was thereafter inextricably bound up with that of his command. Soon after his disastrous defeat at Missionary Ridge (25 November 1863), Bragg resigned his command. Subsequently he served briefly as chief of staff to Jefferson Davis and then commanded a division under Joe Johnston in the Carolinas during the closing weeks of the war. Although he was by no means an incompetent organizer or planner, he lacked flexibility and had serious defects of personality which caused him to lose the confidence of his subordinates.

cause whose instrument he was. It was well that this was so; for his relentless energy, stoked by both dark emotions and shining idealism, was one of the major reasons that the Union armies won the Civil War. So Stanton wanted George Thomas to lead the *Army of the Cumberland* in the grand assault upon the heartland of the foe.

But Mr. Lincoln said no. Once before, at the outset of the Perryville campaign, with Buell clearly losing control of his army, Lincoln and Stanton had decided to replace Buell with Thomas; but methodical Thomas, preferring to start fresh and square in a new command, was disinclined to accept an emergency appointment to lead an army in some ways out of control on the eve of a significant battle, and he refused. The President was not a petty or vindictive man; indeed, he was prepared to bear almost any personal abuse or humiliation if it helped even a mite to put the Rebellion on the road to destruction; but his many years in politics had inculcated in him a strong respect for the quality of loyalty. Effective politics could not be conducted without it, and neither, Mr. Lincoln was coming increasingly to believe, could effective warfare. George Thomas had failed the President when Mr. Lincoln had laid a claim upon his loyalty; a good political leader did not get his will heeded and his works accomplished by rewarding those who lacked loyalty. Moreover, Governor Oliver P. Morton, of Indiana, who single-handedly, through means fair and

foul, lawful and extra-legal, honest and nefarious, was with desperate patriotism keeping his state's staunch soldiers and vital resources strongly committed to the Union cause, had a different, and perhaps better, candidate to replace Buell. So Mr. Lincoln said no. George Thomas would not be given the *Army of the Cumberland*. A petulant loser, which was perhaps just as well for the military interests of the Republic, Stanton was furious. "Well," he said grimly, "you have made your choice of idiots!"

George Henry Thomas.

But Stanton's assessment was far from right. The new commander of the *Army of the Cumberland* was a very able man; a shrewd and tireless thinker who crafted some of the finest battle plans of the Civil War. Had he been just a little more hard-driving, or a little surer tactician, or maybe just a little luckier, he might have been one of the great commanders of the war; but he was none of these things, and so he was destined to become just another might-have-been in a war of many might-have-beens. He was Maj. Gen. William Starke Rosecrans, and he came from the command of a corps in Grant's army.

The tough Western soldiers loved "Old Rosy." A West Pointer who, like too many of the bright officers of the peacetime army of barren frontier posts, had left the service for the more challenging and remunerative world of business and returned to the army at the outset of the Civil War, Rosecrans knew how to appeal to the instincts of soldiers. At Corinth (3–4 October 1862), after his men fought hard to hold off a desperate Rebel charge, "Old Rosy" had swept off his campaign hat, declaring that he must stand bareheaded in the presence of such gallant troops.

William S. Rosecrans was a tall, ruddy, hearty man, with a solid, squarish face, Roman nose, short hair, and narrow, neatly trimmed sideburns and beard. He was known to drink hard, another characteristic of the peacetime frontier army. Outwardly, Rosecrans seemed a simple, bluff, affable, sometimes ebullient, man. He often would move through the army's encampment in the darkness after lights-out until he found a tent with a lantern still glowing from within; then he would whack the tent with the flat of his sword, drawing a torrent of profanity, soon followed by hasty apologies when the men recognized their assailant. Rosecrans would listen to these implausible excuses with a mock, goodnatured dignity, then depart cheerily; behind him, he would hear the heartening sound of his men giggling as they snuffed out the light. Unlike Bragg, the approachable and droll Rosecrans knew how to win the affections of a rough and rude, but also hard-fighting, volunteer army. His men cheered him often, and sang:

> "Old Rosy is our man,
> Old Rosy is our man,
> He'll show his deeds, where'er he leads.
> Old Rosy is our man."

Nevertheless, Rosecrans was anything but what he appeared so clearly to be, a simple, hearty old pro of the Old Army; instead, he was a highly complex, moody, thoughtful man and soldier. Rosecrans in many ways was really a philosopher and teacher. A Cahtolic, he took the many profound mysteries of his faith very seriously. He delighted in late-night seminars with his staff, in which he speculated philosophically on abstruse points of religion and metaphysics. He had ideas on all subjects; some were brilliant insights, others were wrongheaded. He preferred eager, aggressive young officers on his staff because he admired verve, "ginger," he called it, and liked to train his officers to think lucidly. Deeply religious and an intellectual, his knowledge of the nature of man and life often depressed him; he was moody and subject to swift changes of emotion. William S. Rosecrans was a kind of profane saint.

William Starke Rosecrans, commander of the Army of the Cumberland, disliked wasting his men in combat, yet he was involved in two of the bloodiest battles of the entire Civil War: Murfreesboro and Chickamauga.

If Rosecrans had the potential to be a great soldier it was because he was so smart; given sufficient time, he would invariably find the perfect solution to any problem of strategy and tactics. He was a born planner and staff officer; when he had sufficient time, he was a great soldier. But like many men who think deeply, he also thought slowly, wishing to consider all aspects of his dilemma. Often it happens in war that there is not time to think long and deeply; and when that happened to Rosecrans, he was no longer a great soldier. At those times, he was

Henry Wager Halleck, General-in-Chief of the Union armies from 1862 until replaced by Ulysses S. Grant in 1864. While an expert bureaucrat, he was a overly cautious and sometimes inept military commander.

a very mediocre soldier. As Fletcher Pratt once observed, if war were waged on a chessboard, William Stark Rosecrans would have been one of the great commanders in history.

And so the war in Tennessee was to be run by two men who were opposites: Braxton Bragg who was hated by his army and William Starke Rosecrans who was beloved. Braxton Bragg was an inflexible tactician because he thought too little; William Starke Rosecrans was an inflexible tactician because he thought too much.

The men in Washington had replaced Buell because they deemed him lacking in aggressiveness; now they expected his replacement to fight—and soon. Lincoln, Stanton, and the nearest thing the army possessed to a modern chief-of-staff, the large and indecisive Maj. Gen. Henry Wager Halleck—never was a cautious man more inappropriately named—all feared that the Confederate strategists would try to use their interior position to shift the bulk of Bragg's army west in order to build up a crushing concentration against Grant's army along the Mississippi if Rosecrans did not strike the Army of Tennessee promptly. So the concern of the men in Washington was legitimate, even if they did tend to mightily underestimate the complexity of the logistical problem involved in sustaining large armies in the mostly wilderness West. However, in fact they need not have fretted so. Tennessee was much too important to the Confederacy for Davis and his planners to take the great risk of leaving it virtually completely exposed to conquest; Braxton Bragg and his men, eager to take out their mutual frustrations on presumptuous Yankees, would still be there, ready and waiting, when Rosecrans and his boys struck southeast toward Chattanooga.

Rosecrans needed more time, not merely to augment his animals and supply wagons, but also to come up with a plan that he felt comfortable with. He wanted to lull the enemy into a false sense of security and then strike rapidly; but he had not worked it all out yet. The men in Washington were insistent, and Halleck warned Rosecrans early in December of 1862, that he had already been asked twice to name a successor for him. But Rosecrans always won these telegraphic debates by clinging to lofty principles. He wired Halleck: "I need no other stimulus to make me do my duty than the knowledge of what it is. To threats of removal or the like, I must be permitted to say I am insensible." A man who talks like that to his bosses had best be very good indeed at his work. It was time for Rosecrans to show his stuff.

CHAPTER II

MURFREESBORO, DECEMBER 1862–JANUARY 1863

By mid-December of 1862 Bragg's Army of Tennessee and Rosecrans' *Army of the Cumberland* had been relatively inactive for over two months, the former concentrated at Murfreesboro and the latter at Nashville, not 40 miles to the northwest. Though patrols and outposts clashed on a regular basis, both commanders hoarded the bulk of their forces and pressed preparations for a major battle. By late-December each believed he was ready.

All Civil War armies found themselves much depleted when on the offensive if they intended an invasion, as opposed to a raid, because of the need to leave many troops behind to defend major supply bases and railway lines. The railroads were particularly vulnerable to swift Rebel cavalry raids, and when the lines were cut, it was impossible to sustain large numbers of troops in offensive operations. Indeed, one of Grant's first major attempts to capture Vicksburg was defeated by just such a cavalry raid against his railroad supply line. So although Rosecrans' army theoretically numbered about 82,000 men, he moved southeast from Nashville with three corps commanded by Maj. Gens. Thomas L. Crittenden, George H. Thomas, and Alexander McCook, numbering but 44,000 troops, to confront Bragg's army of 34,000 infantry and gunners with 4,000 cavalrymen: Nashville was Rosecrans' supply base, and he had to leave behind a whole division of Thomas' corps to hold it as well as leave thousands more to guard rail lines and junctions, bridges, and smaller supply depots.

Bragg needed to hold Murfreesboro because it was his supply depot. As a result, he did not wish to move too far away from the town even to obtain more tenable defensive ground. He deployed the bulk of his army a little to the northwest of Murfreesboro, on the west bank of Stones River, shallow at that time of year. To the left was Lt. Gen. William J. Hardee's II Corps. Hardee was an experienced, thoughtful soldier who was considered the Old Army's premiere tactician; this led him to believe that he was smarter and abler than he was. It also tended to make him critical of his commander, whom he deemed a clumsy tactician. Fifteen miles eastward was deployed the I Corps of Lt. Gen. Leonidas Polk. Polk was a fiery man, and a religious zealot; an Episcopalian bishop, he possessed a strong commanding presence and courtly ways that made him very popular in the army. He also had powerful political friends. He disliked Bragg for his cold, curt ways and his attempts to shift blame upon others when things did not go well for the army; and he feared that Bragg's clumsy tactics would kill too many of his men, whose affection he reciprocated with a kind of rough, paternal protectiveness. Bragg's corps commanders did not much like giving battle in open farm country without strong natural defenses; nor did they relish Bragg's unwillingness to countenance the digging of defensive works. Bragg wanted to attack.

Rosecrans decided to hit hard at the right flank of the Rebel line with Thomas' and Crittenden's corps and strike straight for Murfreesboro. McCook's job was to feint and/or hold, and if hit hard, to fall back slowly, refusing his flank to protect Thomas' corps on his left.

When Bragg noted McCook's ostentatious preparatory movements, he assumed that the Yankees intended to strike him hard on the left; he determined to get in the first punch in that vicinity. He shifted his reserve division and one from Hardee's corps to assault McCook. Thus, as one historian put it so well, "both commanders had identical plans of battle . . . an advance on the left to strike the enemy's right. . . . if they had moved simultaneously, the two armies might have grappled and swung round and round, like a pair of dancers. . . ." But Bragg's men struck first, at dawn on 31 December.

McCook's corps was half again as strong as the attacking Rebel force, but most of the Union troops were caught at breakfast and overwhelmed before they had much chance to fight. McCook was a West Pointer who had handled a division ably, but this was one of a series of untoward occurrences in his career as a corps commander that would lead him to military oblivion. Two of his divisions disintegrated, losing close to half their numbers. And now Polk's two divisions were sent into the assault. But McCook's third division, with more time to brace themselves, and led firmly by pugnacious Maj. Gen. Philip Henry Sheridan, held their ground and poured torrents of fire into the serried lines of charging Rebels, blasting them back three times. Finally, the second of Polk's divisions, led well and bravely by a tough, profane Tennessean, Maj. Gen. Benjamin Cheatham, supported by Hardee's men, succeeded in driving back the determined union infantry. Cheatham shouted to his troops as he led them in assault, "Give 'em hell, boys!" The prim Bishop Polk, unwilling to appear to sanction profanity even in so good a cause, quickly yelled, "Give them what General Cheatham says, boys! Give them what General Cheatham says!"

Leonidas Polk, a Episcopalian minister turned General, led the I Corps of the Army of Tennessee under Braxton Bragg. Nicknamed the "Fighting Bishop."

Sheridan's loss was heavy in blood, and all three of his brigade commanders went down in the day's fight; but his division's stout resistance in desperate adversity helped give Rosecrans the precious time he needed to avert disaster. He quickly redeployed Crittenden's corps to anchor the Union left, while Thomas' two divisions moved to face west. The Union line was now L-shaped, facing south and west.

Everyone agreed afterward that Rosecrans was magnificent. He rode all over the battlefield, as one officer said, "as firm as iron," encouraging, cajoling, repeating time after time, "This battle must be won." A cannonball ripped away the head of his nearby chief of staff, and spattered his dark blue coat bright red with blood. But on he went, riding hard from unit to unit, looking like a man who had ridden through a slaughterhouse, a dead cigar clenched tightly in his teeth, his black campaign hat firmly on his head, and always reiterating, "This battle must be won."

In one sense, Rosecrans' task was easier than Bragg's. His only course was clear—he had to hold where he was; there was nothing else that he could do. But Bragg, thwarted in his plan to destroy his foe with one powerful blow against a portion of his extended defense line—as all such attempts failed in the Civil War due to the great defensive firepower and infantry mobility of the rifle armies of that war—did not know what to do next.

Bragg then decided to strike the Union line at the junction of Crittenden's and Thomas' corps. On a map this made sense; on the ground, it did not. His crotchety corps commanders were certainly right about one thing; Braxton Bragg had a blind man's eye for terrain. He decided to send Polk's men directly at a clump of rising ground surrounded by a thick forest of cedars. On the maps it was called the Round Forest; the Rebel infantry would refer to it as "Hell's Half-Acre."

Bragg's circumstances were not at strong as they appeared. Hardee's ostensibly victorious units already had been badly mangled this bloody, gray December morning. Hardee had lost one-third of his troops, and already six of his regimental and brigade commanders were down. And Polk's men had suffered, too. The Rebel infantry were brave, but Polk's men were worn, and not as hot for battle as before. Polk worried over the folly of assaulting so strong a position. But orders had to be obeyed.

The Mississippians of Maj. Gen. J. M. Withers' division went forward boldly, yelling as they had at Shiloh. When 50 Yankee cannon blasted

Yankees of the 21 Michigan Infantry. Attached to Philip Sheridan's division, they saw action at both Murfreesboro and Chickamauga and later fought under Sherman during his famous march to the sea.

them from the clump of high ground above the cedars; they lost a lot of men, but still advanced raggedly toward the trees. Then they were staggered by intense sheets of fire from the blueclad infantry concealed in the forest. The Mississippians stopped as if they had run into a stone wall, buckled, and fell back. Ben Cheatham's Tennesseans went in next, gallant men given an impossible task. Bragg lacked the tactical sense to send in the two brigades together, instead of separately; it probably would have made little difference in the end, but his piecemeal assaults had no chance at all. The Tennesseans were shot to pieces, sustaining even more terrible losses than their predecessors. The 16th Tennessee Infantry lost more than 50 percent of its troops. The 8th Tennessee was shattered: 424 of its men had headed through the fields of unpicked cotton in front of the cedar forest and little knob of high ground; only 118 of them made it back. Bishop Polk writhed in remorse and fury at the slaughter of his brave, beloved infantry. He would find it hard to trust Braxton Bragg again.

But Bragg was not yet done. If his assaults were failing, it could not be the fault of his plan; it must be the fault of the men assigned to carry it out. All he needed was to try it again with fresher troops. And luckily, he still had at hand his reserve division, the largest in his army—five brigades—led by Maj. Gen. John C. Breckinridge. Breckinridge, a former Vice-President of the United States, a powerful and influential Kentuckian, was an enthusiastic but not especially gifted soldier.

Bragg should not have sought to reinforce failure; he should have used Breckinridge's men to reinforce Hardee's left and swung them through and around McCook's badly battered outfits hanging on north of Thomas' staunch men. A well-handled assault at that end of the Union line might have smashed right through the Federal army, shattering its flank once again, and also cutting it off from its main line of retreat, the turnpike to Nashville. But Bragg, as ever, was determined to follow his original plan. He ordered Breckinridge's outfit to assault the Round Forest.

Breckinridge demurred. He did not like the idea of leaving Murfreesboro and the Confederate right flank exposed. But Bragg told him to leave one brigade in place and reinforce Polk with the others. Breckinridge's brigades moved out two at a time. When the first pair arrived, Bishop Polk, never brilliant and perhaps a little addled by the disaster to his own men, sent them in without waiting for the rest of

Soldiers of the Army of the Cumberland. Western soldiers were often viewed as less disciplined and crude when compared to their Eastern counterparts in the Army of the Potomac. However, these fighters proved their mettle and determination in some of the bloodiest battles of the war.

Breckinridge's troops to come up. Bragg, unlike Rosecrans, was isolated from the battle for much of the day. This was his style of command; he tended to be satisfied simply to see his plans carried out, and he rarely paid much attention to how they were carried out. He did not intervene to stop Polk's insane piecemeal attacks and make him use Breckinridge's brigades in mass. Once again, the separate tides of gray-clad men were shot and blasted back, leaving a pitiful flotsam of bloody, maimed men in their wake.

Bragg's army could attack no more.

As one historian wrote, "The sun went down . . . and the racket died away. After eleven hours of uproar, a . . . hush fell over the glades and copses, and the brief winter twilight faded into . . . darkness. . . ." It was the last night of the year; and soon a hard, cold rain began to fall.

Bragg thought that he had won; he saw no recourse for Rosecrans but to retreat back down the Nashville pike. And perhaps Rosecrans might have done just that—it is hard to say—but

for two factors. He had reason to believe, incorrectly, that he could not fall back; he feared that the Rebels had already cut the road behind him, and that he was surrounded. The other reason had a name—George H. Thomas. Utterly cool and extremely tenacious in battle, the strapping Virginian spread calm and confidence wherever he tread. When the possibility of retreat was broached, he always muttered grimly the same hard words: "This army doesn't retreat."

Rosecrans did not know what else to do but simply hang on; no one else did either. When he asked luckless McCook—his corps had also been the first routed at Perryville—if he had any advice for the morrow, the latter showed an engaging sardonic grit, replying: "No. Only I would like for Bragg to pay me for my two horses lost today."

Bragg did not know what to do, either. His army was too badly hurt for either he or his corps commanders to have much heart for renewed attacks. But none of them wanted to accept responsibility for a retreat. Bragg hoped

that Rosecrans would retreat; Bragg's corps commanders hoped that Bragg would order a retreat. None of this happened. Rosecrans held in place; Bragg, having assured Richmond that he had won a tactical victory, did not wish to retreat.

The armies spent New Year's Day in relative inactivity. Rosecrans sent a division across the river to hold a hill on the east bank. Bragg was thinking of sending Polk's corps in a renewed assault, but he realized that Polk's men would be badly hurt by enfilade fire from Union guns on the hill. He decided to order Breckinridge's men to take the hill. He understood that it was a tough assignment, so he told Breckinridge to try it just before dark, so that the Yankees would not have time to bring up reinforcements or organize a counter-attack.

But by now Breckinridge had had enough. He protested that the foe had reinforced the hill with two more brigades, and that it was too strongly held; he complained of the difficulty of the terrain, and that the Union guns on the west bank would shred his flank if he tried to advance on the hill. But Bragg had had enough, too. He had not forgiven Breckinridge's reluc-

tance to follow orders on the first day of the battle. He looked hard at Breckinridge and coldly gave him a direct order: "Sir . . . I have given the order to attack the enemy in your front and expect it to be obeyed."

Heartsick, John Breckinridge went to tell his men the orders. Most of them were exiled Kentuckians like himself, so he often referred to them as his "poor orphans." He could hardly bear to face them now. Bitterly, he told one of his brigade commanders, "General Preston, this attack is made against my judgment and by the special orders of General Bragg. Of course we all must try to do our duty and fight the best we can. But if it should result in disaster and I be among the slain, I want you to do justice to my memory and tell the people that I believed this attack to be very unwise and tried to prevent it."

The tough, proud bluegrass infantry had no chance—yet they almost made it. They lunged across the intervening valley, climbed the hill—4,500 angry, desperate men—and drove the Yankee infantry off the crest. And then, from across the river, Crittenden's chief gunner, Capt. John Mendenhall, opened fire with his 58 wisely sited, double-shotted field pieces. A

Union columns deploy into battle at Murfreesboro or Stones River. Murfreesboro was a bloody inconclusive battle fought in the frigid dampness of New Years Eve of 1862. Both armies involved suffered a combined total of almost 25,000 casualties.

storm of steel slashed into the gallant Kentuckians. A Union gunner wrote later: "Thinned, reeling, broken under that terrible hail, the graybacks milled in confusion, scarcely knowing at first what had struck them. . . . The very forest seemed to fall before our fire." The Kentuckians were beaten. A Union colonel wryly noted, "It was difficult to say which was running away the more rapidly, the division of Van Cleve to the rear, or the enemy in the opposite direction."

In an hour and ten minutes, the Kentuckians lost 1,700 of their number. Those who got back found John Breckinridge in tears; and if they could have peered into his soul they would have found there a fierce, burning hatred of Braxton Bragg. It would be hard for hearty, emotional John Breckinridge to entrust his gallant orphans again to the designs of Braxton Bragg.

Finally, Bragg and his commanders decided to retreat, sharing and blurring the responsibility as much as possible. The Army of Tennessee fell back to the rich Duck River Valley to strengthen itself and build a tenable defense line.

The Battle of Murfreesboro was over. At Murfreesboro—also known as Stones River—Bragg lost nearly a third of his army, 11,739 men: 1,294 killed, 7,945 wounded, and about 2,500 captured and missing. Rosecrans' losses were 13,249, about 30% of his army: 1,730 killed, 7,802 wounded, and 3,717 captured or missing. The total of losses was 24,988, greater in this comparatively unknown battle than sustained at bloody Shiloh or Antietam.

Who won? Both sides thought they did. The dauntless Southern infantry believed that they had whipped the Yankee infantry badly, but had suffered heavily, as usual, from the fine Bluecoat artillery. Still, they did not feel much like victors as they marched, worn and miserable, in the icy rain through clinging muck, feeling sorry for themselves, and proud of themselves, at the same time—as veteran combat infantrymen will—grumbling about still another victory, like Perryville, that produced only retreat. They blamed Bragg, wondering, "What does he fight battles for?" And they tried not to get too discouraged—but it was hard.

Rosecrans' men, too, thought they had won; after all, they held the field of battle—it was the Rebels who had retreated. They cheered Rosecrans for his gallantry, and in cheering their leader they were cheering themselves, too; they were coming of age as soldiers. The Secretary of War, who detested Rosecrans as a Democrat and a temporizer, hypocritically lauded him fulsomely: "The country was filled with admiration of the gallantry and heroic achievement of yourself and the officers and troops under your command. . . . There is nothing you can ask within my power to grant to yourself or your noble command that will not be cheerfully given." Even stolid Halleck, so chary of praise, exulted: "You and your brave army have won the gratitude of your country and the admiration of the world. . . . All honor to the Army of the Cumberland. . . ." At that stage in the war, the Union leadership, so used to disaster on the battlefield, thought that a stalemated battle was a victory.

Who won? Neither army, or both armies; but perhaps the edge of decision went to the *Army of the Cumberland*, despite Rosecrans' utter loss of the initiative throughout the battle, a harbinger of future travail for his soldiers. For the Union army had advanced a little ways along the long, hard road to Chattanooga; and Bragg's rigidity and clumsy butcher's tactics had begun to undermine the respect of his army.

But much would depend on what happened next. And what happened next was exactly what had happened to each army in the fall; the recapitulation lasted nearly half a year, and its results were, at least at first, much better for one army than the other.

Previous Page: *Yankees of the 78th Pennsylvania and 21st Ohio storm and seize a Confederate battery on the second day of Murfreesboro. Bragg had driven his army to the point of exhaustion, but failed to follow up his successes. He wasted the lives of thousands of his soldiers for no purpose when the Confederacy was desperate for fighting men.*

CHAPTER III

LULL, JANUARY–JUNE 1863

In the aftermath of Murfreesboro, the Army of Tennessee was to be granted the longest reprieve from battle of any Confederate army during the Civil War. But this most precious asset, time, was wasted. Bragg and his commanders did not use it to plan a coherent strategy for the defense of Tennessee or to build a strong defense line to protect Chattanooga; instead, they squandered this asset in bitter, futile recrimination.

Aloof and dour, Bragg did not make friends readily, nor did he possess sufficient understanding of human nature to be able to inspire and manipulate others to make his purposes their own; a cold bureaucrat, he understood rules, but not people, and thus found it difficult to deal with individuals. Had his battlefield performance been better, much of this would have been forgiven; but to his officers and men, Bragg seemed hypocritical, demanding of them standards of excellence which he did not demand of himself. They saw him as indecisive in strategy and rigid in tactics, a ferocious martinet in camp and wasteful of their lives in battle. They damned him as a man who won tactical victories—and then invariably retreated. "Why does he fight battles?" they asked, mockingly.

To Bragg, his officers were disloyal and insubordinate, and his troops lacked the staunchness of those in other Confederate armies. He responded to criticism with abuse and threats. As the leading scholar of the Army of Tennessee well and truly wrote: "Bragg never understood that his army was a series of cliques, each based around some general with a regional or personal attraction. Each of his corps and division leaders . . . had a cadre of surrounding officers and staff members. In turn, these groups were often backed by geographical combines. . . . To these men, preserving face was all important. Bragg never realized this. . . . he

publicly humiliated his generals. . . ." He did not understand "that the sentiment against him . . . was widespread. . . . he tossed it off as the handiwork of only several disgruntled officers [who] . . . were only trying to hide their own faults. Thus, Bragg considered this discontent to be a passing thing which could be eliminated by punishment of the particular dissenter. He did not seem to understand that a strike against Cheatham would be considered an affront not only to Polk but also to the proud Tennessee troops. An attack . . . on Breckinridge would involve other Kentucky officers."

Bragg and his commanders soon became absorbed in a bitter paper war over who bore the greatest responsibility for the retreat from Murfreesboro; and it soon became clear that Bragg had lost the confidence of almost all of the general officers of his army. They wanted a new commanding officer. And they almost got one. Jefferson Davis asked Gen. Joseph E. Johnston to investigate the strange circumstances of Bragg's army. But the diffident Johnston observed only outward appearances: Bragg's army was well-fed and -clothed, healthy, and in good condition. Johnston admired Bragg's efficiency; and he felt sorry for the stern, cadaverous North Carolinian whose ailments and taut nerves made him seem on the thin edge of complete physical and emotional breakdown. The prim Johnston who scorned the role of executioner of the career of an honest and efficient officer, decided to let the politicians do their own dirty work. Joe Johnston protected Bragg.

In the spring, some of the Confederate leadership gave passing thought to sending imposing reinforcements to Bragg's army, thus shifting the entire focus of the Confederacy's strategy in the war. It was proposed to use the South's advantage of interior lines to transfer strong forces from Virginia, to allow Bragg to build up, through this rapid concentration, a strong preponderance over Rosecrans' army and thus defeat the Union forces and drive them from Tennessee. But Lee would not hear of it—he was planning to take the offensive, and thus needed all of his troops ready at hand. The choice of whether to entrust the shining hope of a Confederate summer offensive to the capable, successful hands of Lee and his confident army or to entrust what might well prove the climactic campaign of the war to the uninspired, unsuccessful Bragg and his depressed, bitterly divided army was, of course, really no choice at all. One reinforces success, not failure. Lee retained all of his troops.

And so the Army of Tennessee wasted its six months' respite from battle.

But the *Army of the Cumberland* did not—although this was not to be evident for some time.

Rosecrans, too had a familiar problem. The men in Washington were prodding him to exploit his dubious victory at Murfreesboro, to attack Bragg's army again, and drive it from Chattanooga and beyond. But Rosecrans bided his time; he needed many more wagons and animals to supply his army on the offensive, and he bluntly told Halleck, "I believe the most fatal errors of this war have begun in an impatient desire of success, that would not take time to get ready." When the pragmatic Halleck, un-

Henry Halleck (1815–1872)

A native of New York, Halleck ran away from home rather than take up farming and was eventually adopted by his maternal grandfather, who saw to it that he received an excellent education (Phi Beta Kappa, Union College). At West Point he was assigned as an assistant professor even before graduating third in the class of 1839. He became an engineer and helped design the harbor defenses of New York before touring French coast defenses in 1844. He wrote several important works, including *Report on the Means of National Defense* and *Elements of Military Art and Science*, and translated Henri Jomini's *Political and Military Life of Napoleon* from the French. He saw administrative service in California during the Mexican War, emerging with a brevet, and later served as inspector and engineer of lighthouses on the Pacific Coast, as well as on the board proposing fortifications for the Pacific Coast. Meanwhile he found time to help frame the Constitution of the State of California and study law. In 1854 he resigned from the army and founded a major law firm in California. Refusing a judgeship and a

Henry W. Halleck.

U.S. Senate seat, Halleck devoted himself to his profession, to writing, to business, and to the state militia, becoming an authority on mining and international law and quite wealthy in the process. At the outbreak of the war he was appointed a major general in the Regular Army at the suggestion of Winfield Scott. Great things were

expected of Halleck, but he proved an inept field commander. This fact took some time to become apparent; when he commanded in the West in 1862 his subordinates included Ulysses S. Grant and William S. Rosecrans. Appointed General-in-Chief of the army in July of 1862, Halleck's great administrative abilities proved immensely valuable. Despite the fact that he acted more as a clerk-in-chief than a general-in-chief, he did much to promote a more efficient organization of the army and managed to keep the troops supplied and reinforcements forthcoming, but could have done far more to coordinate the activities of the Union armies. In early 1864 he was replaced by Grant and demoted to the status of Chief-of-Staff, a task which he performed to perfection. After the war he held various administrative posts until his death. Halleck's old army nickname "Old Brains," conferred in recognition of his great intellectual achievements, was eventually replaced by "Old Wooden Head." Had there never been a war he might have remained a soldier of great promise, rather than a great disappointment.

Federals pass the time during the lull in action in the west during the late winter and spring of 1863, blissfully unaware of the bloody battle looming in their future.

William S. Rosecrans (1819–1898)

William Starke Rosecrans.

A native of Ohio, the staunchly Catholic Rosecrans graduated West Point fifth in the Class of 1838, entering the prestigious Corps of Engineers. His military service, entirely administrative, ended in 1854, when he went into business as a civil engineer and architect. On the outbreak of the Civil War he was appointed a brigadier in the Regular Army and served with some distinction in western Virginia (Rich Mountain, 11 July 1861). He later led a division with skill at Corinth (22–30 May 1862) and then the *Army of the Mississippi* at Iuka (19 September 1862) and Corinth (3–4 October 1862). Given command of the *Army of the Cumberland* on 27 October 1862, Rosecrans led it at Murfreesboro (31 December 1862–2 January 1863), and all through the Chickamauga Campaign until relieved on 19 October. During 1864 he commanded the *Department of Missouri*, but was effectively unemployed thereafter, eventually resigning from the service in 1867, after over two years of inactivity. In subsequent years Rosecrans served briefly as minister to Mexico (1868), Representative from California (1881–1885), and Register of the Treasury (1885–1893). An excellent organizer and brilliant planner, Rosecrans was meticulous about logistical matters. In battle, however, he was slow to react and unlucky.

able to threaten an apparently successful general with removal, offered Rosecrans a much coveted, high promotion for "an important and decisive victory," he merely elicited a pompous and overly righteous response: "As an officer and a citizen, I feel degraded to see such auctioneering of honor. Have we a general who would fight for his own personal benefit when he would not for honor and the country? He would . . . deserve to be despised by men of honor." Halleck, his ample patience sorely tried by Rosecrans' insolent procrastination, admonished Old Rosy that the expense of these frequent telegraphic communications between him and Washington was threatening to undermine the Union's military budget!

The men in Washington were frantic with fear that Rosecrans' lethargy would allow the Rebels to detach forces from Bragg's army and achieve a strong concentration to defeat Grant's army at Vicksburg. So they threatened to take troops away from Rosecrans and send them to reinforce Grant unless the *Army of the Cumberland* promptly took the offensive.

Finally, toward the end of June—a week short of six months from the first day at Murfreesboro—the *Army of the Cumberland* moved south. It proved to be a move well worth waiting for; for given sufficient time, there were few better commanders than the thoughtful William Starke Rosecrans.

The Federal camp at Murfreesboro. Both the Army of the Cumberland and the Army of Tennessee had several months of rest after Murfreesboro. Encampments took on a permanent look as soldiers thought the war might pass them by without another battle — they were sadly mistaken.

CHAPTER IV

THE TULLAHOMA OPERATION, JUNE–JULY 1863

When the *Army of the Cumberland* resumed its advance south in late June of 1863, it was clear that Rosecrans had spent his time wisely. Impressed by the bloodshed—and the close proximity of disaster—at Stones River, Rosecrans did not this time intend to march straight down the main roads toward a frontal battle with Bragg's army. He intended to carry out that rarest of Civil War maneuvers, a successful turning movement, or flank attack. This is why he had mercilessly dunned Halleck and his reluctant quartermasters for so many animals and wagons; he was going to need them to supply his army off the main roads. And he was shrewd enough to perceive that the broken, wild country north of the Duck River, so "full of natural passes and fortifications," as he had told Halleck, was more an advantage to his army than a disadvantage; he intended that the wooded ridges would screen the flanking movement of his army from Bragg's forces blocking the passes astride the main roads. It was a thoughtful, even brilliant, but also hazardous, plan; much depended upon the element of surprise. Rosecrans would have to divide his army more than he liked in order to move rapidly in bad country, and if the Rebels were perceptive and alert, and able to move rapidly, they might be able to concentrate the bulk of their forces against portions of his divided army and defeat the *Army of the Cumberland* in detail. But his plan was so good that it was a risk well worth accepting. Leaving about 22,500 soldiers behind to protect supply points in the rear, the *Army of the Cumberland* at last moved south in the early morning hours of 24 June with 65,137 troops.

But Old Rosy need not have worried. Braxton Bragg was not an imaginative soldier. Ill and preoccupied, and not able to think very clearly, Bragg and his mediocre subordinate commanders had disposed their 41,680 men to block the way south along the best roads facing the easiest terrain—the obvious route for the Yankees to take when they at last came on. Polk's I Corps was deployed in front of Shelbyville, and Hardee's II Corps in front of Wartrace, both on the north bank of the Duck River, facing the main roads and widest gaps in the tangled, wooded ridges to the north. But Bragg's inappropriate dispositions were not fully of his own doing. His army was pinned widely, extending north of the Duck instead of being better concentrated on more tenable ground, because of its need for food and forage. Confederate quartermasters unwisely allocated much of the produce of Tennessee to Lee's Army of Northern Virginia, leaving Bragg's men on short rations; and the Army of Tennessee's supply of animals, depleted through campaign losses, was hard to maintain due to Federal control of Missouri, Kentucky, and northern Tennessee. Hence, the army's deployment along the Duck was dictated by a combination of bad tactics and bad logistics. Moreover, Bragg and his commanders had not worked out an agreed plan of what to do when Rosecrans finally struck. Bragg had the vague idea that Hardee's corps should try to stem the Yankee advance, while Polk's divisions struck the Bluecoats from the western flank. But Polk was ignorant of this nebulous design. Hardee worried that the right flank of his corps dribbled off into nothingness in the wild, primitive forests and hills to the east; no one told him what to do in the unlikely event that Yankee infantry came pouring out of that feral landscape onto his naked right flank. He assumed he was to fall back across the Duck to the main road and rail junction of Tullahoma. Thus, the legacy of six months of command chaos now doomed the Army of Tennessee before it even fought. This was the situation when Rosecrans made his move.

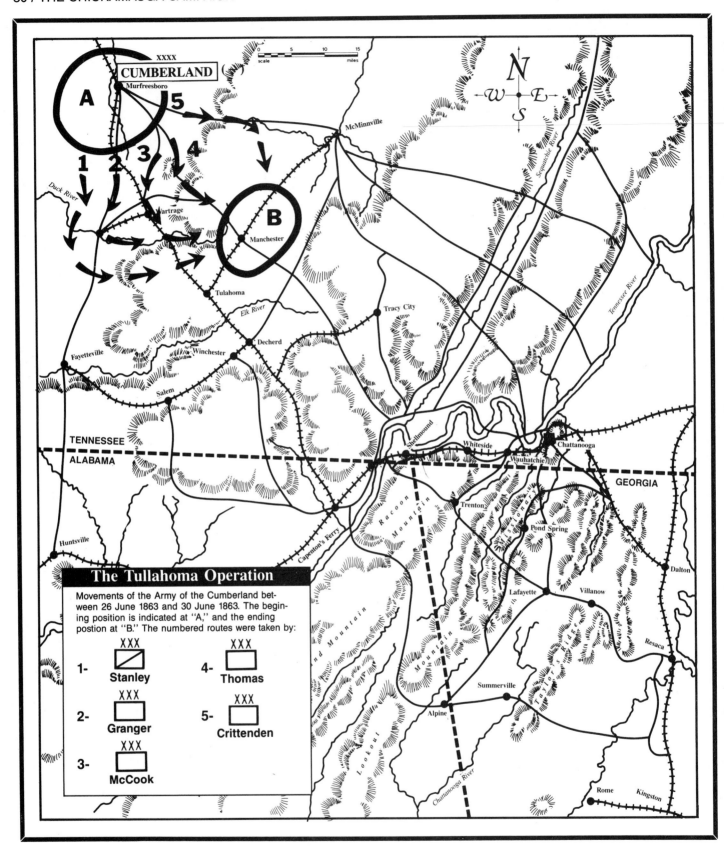

The Tullahoma Operation

Movements of the Army of the Cumberland between 26 June 1863 and 30 June 1863. The beginning position is indicated at "A," and the ending postion at "B." The numbered routes were taken by:

1- Stanley

2- Granger

3- McCook

4- Thomas

5- Crittenden

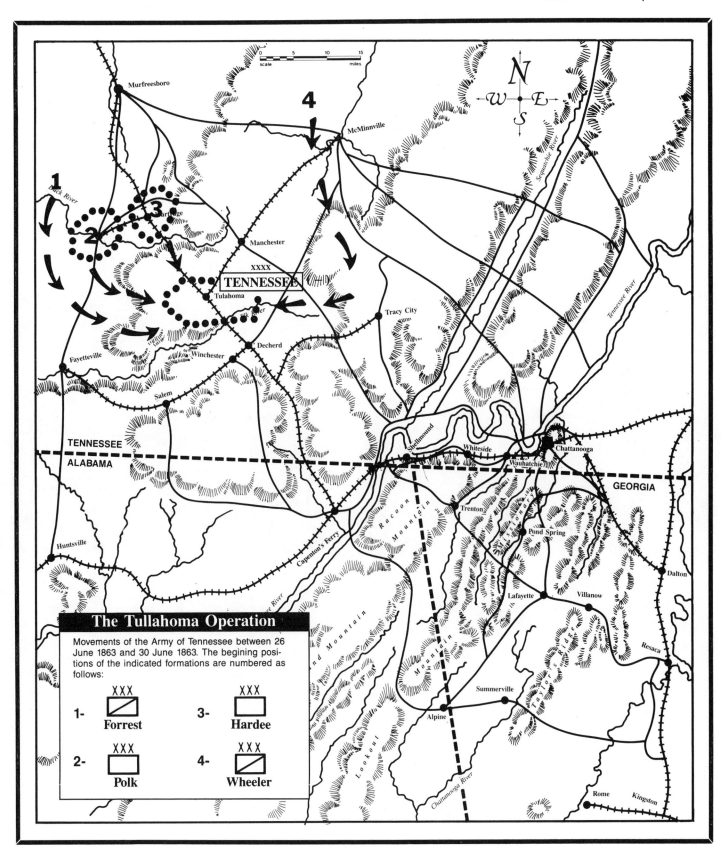

The Tullahoma Operation

Movements of the Army of Tennessee between 26 June 1863 and 30 June 1863. The begining positions of the indicated formations are numbered as follows:

1- XXX Forrest

2- XXX Polk

3- XXX Hardee

4- XXX Wheeler

Maj. Gen. Gordon Granger, commanding Rosecrans' *Reserve Corps* was a tough, self-reliant, hard-edged Regular Army soldier, well suited to independent command. Granger sent his troops barreling down the main routes to Shelbyville to overrun the outposts of the good Bishop Polk and badly worry both him and his cantankerous boss, Braxton Bragg. One of Maj. Gen. Alexander McCook's *XX Corps* divisions struck toward Wartrace to pin Hardee's corps. And all the while, George Thomas' massive *XIV Corps* of four divisions swung wide to the east, marching grimly through drenching, warm spring rains that soaked them wet to their skins—sodden, mud-stained boots splashing through thin muck, relentlessly, endlessly, marching in the dripping woods to get behind the exposed flank of Hardee's vulnerable corps. They got a big boost at the very outset when Col. John T. Wilder's Indiana and Illinois mounted infantrymen rushed straight ahead, without worrying about ambushes in terrain

perfect for such, through the narrow, three-mile long pass known as Hoover's Gap; and then held it against a Rebel counter-attack until Thomas' lead regiments arrived to succor them and push on.

Bragg, desperately concerned with the western end of his line, and oblivious to the threat from the east, as always when needing a rapid decision, reverted to his original scheme. He wanted Hardee's units to strike and pin McCook's outfit north of Wartrace, while Polk's troops drove back Granger's men and then swung eastward to crush the Yankees in front of Hardee from the flank. Polk, as he often did, deemed the enemy too strong; Bragg, as he always did, insisted on his plan. And then Bragg learned that Thomas' hard-marching infantry were headed straight for Manchester, well to the east, and already well behind the Confederate front. The Army of Tennessee had to retreat—and fast.

But hasty retreats are the sire of confusion;

Federal artillerists drill in camp.

At right: *Reb soldiers relax between duties. The morale of the Army of Tennessee was sapped by the uninspiring leadership of Braxton Bragg, turmoil within its leadership, and the constant retreats from June to September. However, when the time came to fight, the Confederates displayed their customary bravery and tenacity.*

Opposite page: *A Union wagon train carrying the necessary supplies for the Army of the Cumberland slogs its way through a \mountain pass. Rosecrans miraculously outflanked and pursued the Army of the Tennessee over mountainous terrain in heavy rain.*

and hasty retreats and confusion in an army whose leaders do not trust one another produce chaos. The units of the Army of Tennessee fell back aimlessly; Bragg, indecisive—changing his mind frequently in the course of the retreat—seemed dazed and ill. No attempt was made to concentrate Rebel forces and strike at the separated Yankee units in pursuit, advancing across rivers and the grain of rough country.

Polk and Hardee were reluctant to commit their troops to battle under Bragg in his parlous condition of physical and emotional health. Bragg was not willing to risk in battle his wary, troubled army with the unfordable Tennessee River at its back. Thus, the army continued its desultory retreat all the way to the east bank of the Tennessee.

As one historian has noted: "The collapse of the Duck River line was the result of months of command instability which . . . produced a paralysis in Bragg's high command. . . . the army's command system just ceased to function."

Rosecrans' bloodless Tullahoma campaign, achieved at the light cost of less than a hundred

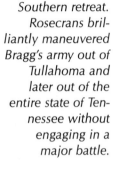

A caricature of the Southern retreat. Rosecrans brilliantly maneuvered Bragg's army out of Tullahoma and later out of the entire state of Tennessee without engaging in a major battle.

dead, a little over 450 wounded, and a dozen missing, was a little known masterpiece of Civil War strategy. In eleven days of maneuver (23 June–4 July), he drove his foe from highly tenable ground, conquered the approaches to the key city of Chattanooga, and inflicted four times his own losses upon the enemy army. The campaign showed what a fine commander Rosecrans was—as long as he had the luxury of sufficient time to think and plan.

But Rosecrans had not destroyed Bragg's army, nor had he yet captured Chattanooga. So it could not have surprised him much after his great, but somewhat unappreciated victory, to have the men in Washington resume their ceaseless, remorseless nagging that he finish the job, taking Chattanooga and destroying Bragg's army. But Rosecrans demurred; he needed more time. And Halleck, frustrated, then touchy, became insistent, finally warning grimly: "I have communicated to you the wishes of the Government in plain and unequivocal terms."

Rosecrans took six weeks, then moved his army south on 16 August. And he produced another strategic masterpiece.

CHAPTER V

ROSECRANS TAKES CHATTANOOGA, AUGUST–SEPTEMBER 1863

To the Rebels, Chattanooga seemed an impregnable bastion, screened by the wild, winding, wide Tennessee River and overlooked by dominating mountains and ridges. As one Rebel officer later said, ". . . when your . . . general . . . commenced his forward movement for the capture of Chattanooga, we laughed him to scorn. We believed that . . . he would dash himself to pieces against the many and vast natural barriers that rise all around Chattanooga, and that then the northern people and the government at Washington would perceive how hopeless were their efforts when they came to attack the real South." And this formidable barrier position would have to be approached over rough, narrow mountain roads and through broken, feral country deficient in food, fodder, and even water.

Yet the position of the Confederate army was not as strong as appeared. The Army of Tennessee was despondent, still brooding over lost battles and torn by personal conflicts; Bragg was unsure of himself and heartsick. "I am utterly broken down," he admitted. The rifts and hatreds in its leadership rendered command and control of the army in battle moot. And it was faced with a highly complex defensive problem due to its loss of the initiative after Murfreesboro; Rosecrans' troops could strike at any one or several of the numerous points at which the Tennessee might be crossed, so that Bragg's army had to watch a frontage of a hundred miles, and it could not be everywhere. Once again, the Army of Tennessee would commence a battle without a generally agreed-upon plan of concentration, and thus once again, it would be defeated before it fought.

And once again, thoughtful William Starke

Rosecrans intended to take the obvious course and reverse it in order to perplex his unimaginative and depressed foes. Rosecrans' best method seemed to be to strike northeast and try to cross the Tennessee in the vicinity of Chattanooga, the key objective. This was the most direct course, and it had the additional advantage of carrying Rosecrans' army closer to the Union army corps of Maj. Gen. Ambrose E. Burnside, operating against Knoxville, to the northeast; the Confederate strategists greatly feared such a junction. But Rosecrans disliked this course of action. He deemed it too obvious, and did not like the fact that it would take his army too far from his southeast-running supply line. He decided to move westward instead, crossing the Tennessee far downstream of Chattanooga, to surprise Bragg's army.

Rosecrans deployed three infantry brigades ostentatiously to the north and northeast of Chattanooga. They lighted bonfires at night, and by day pounded with hammers on empty barrels and threw wood scraps into the water system to simulate the construction of boats for an amphibious assault. Then on 21 August, a Yankee battery began to drop artillery rounds from the high ground across the river directly into the city. Bragg completed his army's concentration at Chattanooga.

On that very day, fifty miles downstream, at Bridgeport, Alabama, a shade south of the Tennessee line, the men of Thomas' *XIV Corps* were tramping across pontoon bridges, marching hard once again in flank and rear of Bragg's army. Crittenden's *XXI Corps* crossed ten miles north, at Shellmound, Tennessee, while McCook's *XX Corps* crossed a dozen miles south, at Caperton's Ferry, Alabama. If Bragg hesitated

COMMAND AND CONTROL IN CIVIL WAR ARMIES

Few—if any—first-rate American field armies have ever been as badly out of the control of its command leadership as Braxton Bragg's Army of Tennessee in the Chickamauga Campaign. This is often ascribed to Bragg's acerbic personality. Yet this is, at best, an incomplete explanation and, at worst, an horrendous oversimplification of a deeply-rooted, complex, and widespread phenomenon in the armies of the Civil War. For failure of command and control was the greatest flaw of the tactical leadership of the Civil War; high commanders proved much too often unable to control the battlefield movements of subordinate units in accordance with their plans. Bragg's failure was simply one of degree—he completely lost control of his army—not one of kind. Lee was a tactical genius, yet loss of command and control marred one of his greatest victories, that of Second Manassas, and ensured that it would be just another dead-end battle, and helped bring about disaster at Gettysburg (1–3 July 1863). The problem was endemic in the *Army of the Potomac*, as exemplified in the disasters to John Pope and Ambrose Burnside in 1862; and even the more professional McClellan was defeated at Antietam because he was unable to coordinate his assaults, allowing his numerically inferior foe to beat off his attacks in detail. Of course, loss of command and control occurs in every war as a result of what Clausewitz called the normal "friction" of war; yet it seems clear that the problem was much more prevalent in the American Civil War than in prior or later wars. It also seems evident that the causes of this went beyond the personal inadequacies

of individual commanders—after all, the Civil War produced many of the very greatest commanders in the annals of American military history—and derived instead from the nature of the armies of the Civil War.

One very important factor in this loss of command and control came with the advent of the rifled musket. As noted, the rifle altered tactical formations, spreading the infantry out in looser, more flexible lines, rather than in the massed, close-order ranks of the age of the smooth-bore musket. This change

allowed greater infantry mobility and flexibility, but necessarily resulted in diminished command and control capability. Doubtless, too, the heavier defensive firepower of riflemen took a larger toll of the attackers who exposed themselves most aggressively—the line officers and noncoms in combat leadership slots—so that offensive units progressively lost tactical responsiveness due to heavy attrition of leadership and eventually buckled. So the rifle was one important factor in undermining traditional elements of command

Confederate troops parade without proper uniforms in Fort McRee. Bragg commanded the fort against Union attack in 1861.

necessitated widespread dispersal of forces. It was essentially a small-unit army, an army primarily of companies; occasionally, a battalion or even a regiment might be put together to operate briefly as an entity in response to a special crisis, but the component units would soon be dispersed again. There were, of course, no divisions or corps, almost never a brigade. The officers learned to command and control small units. They had no inkling—not the slightest—of how to command and control the large units they would be suddenly expected to handle in the Civil War.

Of course, men do not learn only from direct, personal experience (although war is the hardest profession to learn any other way); they also may learn indirectly, from the experience of others, which is through education. Unfortunately, West Point was an excellent school of military—and other—engineering and gunnery, but its rigid and narrow curriculum offered scant insight into the art of the warrior and the history of warfare. In the army, advanced, specialized schools did not yet exist, stifling professional education. The people of the nation as a whole disliked the study of war—perhaps thinking that if it was not thought about and prepared for it would never occur!—and disliked even more the spending of public funds on anything more militarily cerebral than shooting at Indians. The political leaders distrusted military specialization as a potential threat to full civilian control of the Army. And the conditions of army service on the frontier—small knots of mostly idle officers, bored and restless, cut off from the intellectual stimulation to be derived from frequent contact with others of their profession, unable to discuss comman problems or share ideas, unable to build in this way coherent army doctrine—were stultifying to professional growth.

As befit an army of small units, staffs were small and their work

and control in Civil War armies.

Also, it should not be overlooked that much of the Civil War, especially in the West, was fought in a very rural, almost wilderness land, amid desolate broken country and dense woodlands. In this type of terrain, problems of command and control were intensified and magnified. Indeed, one of the great unrecognized problems of Bragg and his corps commanders in the Chickamauga Campaign was that often, because of the terrain, they were uncertain of exactly where Rosecrans' units were, and indeed,

sometimes even of the whereabouts of all of their own units. Much of Bragg's alleged tactical timidity in the time before Longstreet joined him, and his failure to hit Rosecrans' divided forces harder at that time, stemmed from this factor. Bragg was never really sure where Rosecrans' units were.

Another significant factor was the nature of service in the peacetime professional Army of the United States. The pre-war army's primary roles: for the infantry and cavalry, frontier defense, for the artillery coast defense—were roles which

simple. Different procedures and practices evolved in response to small, dispersed commands working out individual problems largely in isolation; there was no army doctrine. The thinking officers who tried to educate themselves in their profession studied the wars of the past and developed ideas suited to them; but then they would be asked to fight the first great rifle war, and they found that the old ideas did not work any more. Even battle experience in the Mexican War (1846–1848) did not help much. The engineers and gunners, reflecting the strengths of West Point, did well, and some even learned how to do better in the future (Lee, Thomas), but others learned little (Bragg). The infantrymen and horse soldiers learned little, because the war was fought with the tactics of the musket. They would be left to learn the lessons of the age of the rifle the hard way and at high price.

So the nature of service in the peacetime professional army did not develop in the tactical leaders of the Civil War the aptitude for command and control of large units in modern battle.

A final factor in the lack of command and control in the Civil War armies was that so many of the officers on both sides were amateurs, essentially civilians, in outlook and psychology. Orders were not always necessarily considered to be binding, just as in the individualistic society as a whole standards of family and societal discipline were more permissive than in older, more structured and authoritarian societies. In America, everyone thought that he knew best, including most army officers. Inexperienced—and therefore sloppy—staffs augmented this trend by producing a torrent of unclear, ambiguous, and discretionary tactical orders that too often left subordinates to do as they pleased.

It should also be noted that the looser formations of the rifle armies and the wooded terrain of much of America at that time were relentlessly destructive of communications—and thus battlefield command and control—in an era before field telephones and radio. Communication was personal and human, via a staff officer with a written or verbal message direct from commander to subordinate. The possibilities of error in such a system—due to officers getting lost, lack of clarity and precision in writing and speech, due to fatigue and tension, and a variety of other human factors—were enormous and frequent, and very much in evidence during the Chickamauga Campaign.

There were many examples of command problems. Hard-fighting but stubborn James Longstreet invariably delayed so long in carrying out orders that he deemed unwise that his doubts usually became self-fulfilling prophecies. Fitzjohn Porter could not serve in peace with John Pope. Union general Jefferson C. Davis shot a fellow general to death during an altercation in a Louisville hotel. And during the Chickamauga Campaign Bragg's army was ultimately paralyzed through loss of command and control—and personality conflicts among—by the army's leaders.

At left: *The Clinch Rifles on May 10, the day before they joined a regiment destined to fame.* Above: *Henry Howe Cook, promoted at age 17 to lieutenant, inspired the sculptor of a Baltimore monument.*

to convert his critics. He became as isolated from his officers as Captain Queeg ever was in the wardroom of the *Caine.* Yet to illlustrate the dimension of the problem, when Hood eventually assumed command of the Army of Tennessee in mid-1864, he had exactly the same difficulty with his subordinates that Bragg had had.

In general, it would seem that the Southerners suffered from this defect more than the Northerners, or even the highly individualistic Westerners. The Southerners were products of a more sparsely populated, very rural society. Men grew up with more space between them, and it was not as necessary for each to cooperate with another in order to achieve goals. They were used to getting their way and more prideful of their honor; perhaps the existence of slavery added to their haughtiness and imperious style. The more crowded and urban males of the North and West had closer neighbors, on nearby farms and city streets and factories; for the most part, they had to cooperate more closely with others to see their endeavors crowned with success, so they were less full of themselves. Certainly if city dwellers challenged each other to duels each time one of the numerous vexations of urban life occurred, the adult male population of the North would have been very small indeed. In any event, it seems likely that the different sectional temperaments worked slightly to the advantage of the Union forces and more to the detriment of the Confederate forces during the Civil War.

Certainly, then, tactical command and control was the major flaw of the Civil War armies, a flaw that was not so much the fault of individual failure, but rather a product of the very nature and composition of those armies and, indeed, in some ways, of the psychology of American society in general at that time.

A stern martinet, Bragg was too rigid to lead a largely volunteer army. The volunteer officers hated his unthinking discipline and resented his clumsy tactics, which resulted in the deaths of too many of their men. They learned to sabotage their chief's orders. Hardee, a veteran professional, thought himself smarter and a far better tactician than Bragg, and hence was slow to carry out—and fast to obstruct—the plans of his leader. Bragg lacked the imagination to appreciate soldiers different from himself and he lacked the tactical skills to win the victories necessary

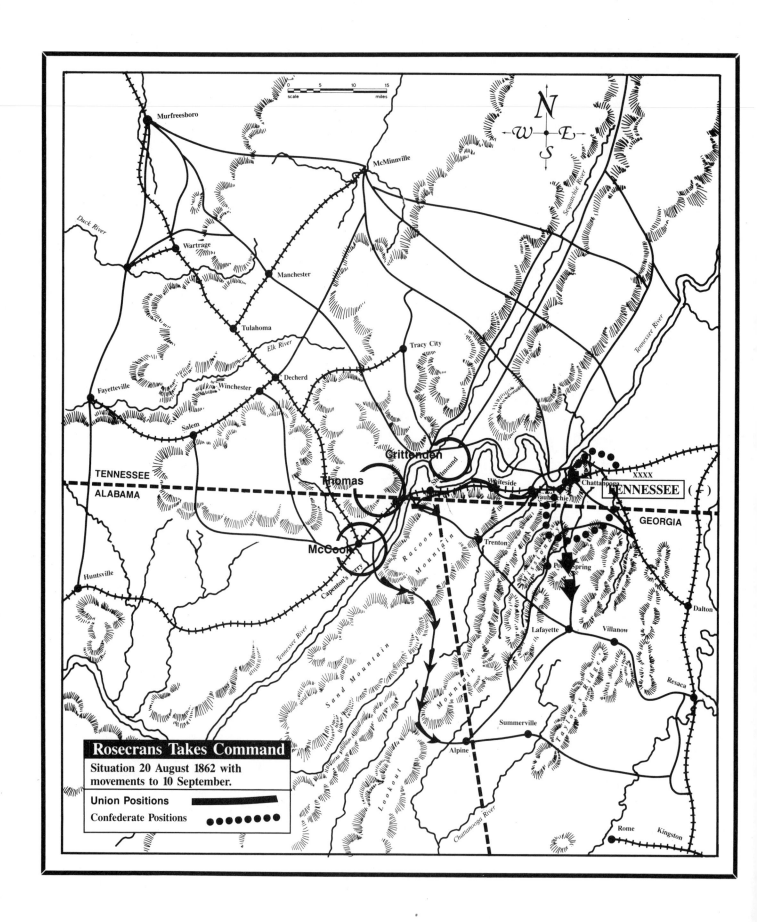

Rosecrans Takes Command

Situation 20 August 1862 with
movements to 10 September.

Union Positions

Confederate Positions

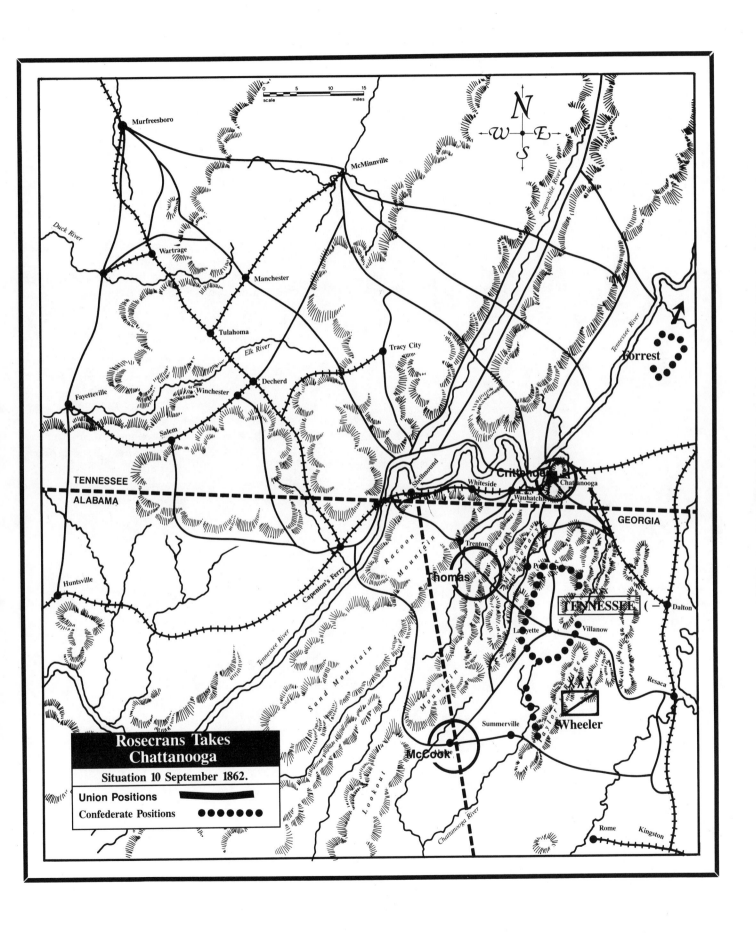

Rosecrans Takes Chattanooga

Situation 10 September 1862.

Union Positions

Confederate Positions

long at Chattanooga, Rosecrans' *Army of the Cumberland* would sweep north, in behind the Army of Tennessee and trap it against the river, just as relentless Sam Grant had pinned the Rebels against the Mississippi not long ago at Vicksburg.

The terrain was high and wild, but when they crossed the Tennessee, Rosecrans' men were well supplied with ammunition and carried three weeks worth of rations; and as always, Rosecrans had them even better supplied with ideas. He had formed special, company-size units equipppped with strong, long ropes to help faltering animals haul cannon and supply wagons up steep mountain grades.

As the hard-marching western Yankees pounded up the high ground, sweating in the summer heat, they saw grand vistas. An Illinois infantryman wrote, "Far beyond mortal vision extended one vast panorama of mountains, forests, and rivers. The broad Tennessee below us seemed like a ribbon of silver; beyond rose the Cumberlands, which we had crossed. The valley on both sides was alive with the moving armies of the Union, while almost the entire transportation of the army filled the roads and fields along the Tennessee. No one could survey the grand scene on that bright autumn [sic] day unmoved, unimpressed with its grandeur and the meaning conveyed by the presence of the mighty host."

Braxton Bragg and his befuddled commanders certainly understood the significance of the long blue columns marching free and unop-posed in the rear of the Army of Tennessee. Bragg's army had no recourse but to retreat south, fleeing east of the high mountains beyond Chattanooga, finally coming to rest again after yet another hasty retreat in the vicinity of LaFayette, Georgia.

William Starke Rosecrans, unbeatable with time to think and plan, had wrought another masterpiece of strategy; he had taken Chattanooga, and it proved an easy thing. And this time he did not intend to stop. The *Army of the Cumberland* headed purposefully into the gaps in the high mountains. This time, Rosecrans needed no urging from the men in Washington. He fully intended to destroy the Confederate army of Braxton Bragg, somewhere up ahead of the darkly wooded and violet dappled high mountains. The Army of Tennessee seemed done.

But Rosecrans would find a different Confederate army waiting for him on the other side of the high mountains in the dense green woodlands of northwest Georgia. The Army of Tennessee was far from done. Braxton Bragg suddenly awoke, as if out of a nightmare, from his torpor of indecisiveness; his resolve grew as he formulated a plan to reverse the fortunes of his army and destroy the overextended *Army of the Cumberland*. And, in addition, Bragg's army was about to receive much help from proud and powerful friends from the Eastern army.

Yankees before the "Indian Mound" in Chattanooga, Tennessee. In August Rosecrans took the strategically vital city of Chattanooga without a fight. Less than a month later, the Yankees found themselves besieged by the same Rebels they had defeated earlier.

CHAPTER VI

BRAGG ESSAYS AN OFFENSIVE, 9–19 SEPTEMBER 1863

After taking Chattanooga, Rosecrans hoped to catch his retreating foe strung-out, and thus subject to ready destruction in detail. But in order to achieve this he had to move forward rapidly. In order to move fast through the gaps in the mountains with a large army, it was necessary for him to divide his forces. Crittenden's corps, to the north, marched toward Rossville Gap; in the center, Thomas' corps marched through Stevens' Gap, toward McLemore's Cove; and in the south, McCook's men marched through Winston Gap, toward Alpine, Georgia. When the three corps finally reached the other side of the mountains they would be widely separated, dispersed over nearly fifty miles of rough country, each corps potentially vulnerable to a concentration of Bragg's entire army against it.

Rosecrans understood the potential vulnerability of his divided army, but was willing to accept the risk in order to have a chance to destroy Bragg's army, which he had defeated twice in as many months, but yet had been unable to bring to decisive battle. Besides, he had divided his forces in the Tullahoma campaign, and all had worked out very well indeed; and he was sure that Bragg's army was by now demoralized, lacking the will to take the offensive and fight hard. But Rosecrans was wrong.

While Braxton Bragg was lacking in imagination, like many suspicious men, he was capable of cunning. In his retreat from Chattanooga, Bragg sent bogus deserters straggling back toward the Yankee lines to be captured—and to tell the Union staff officers just what they knew their boss wanted and expected to hear, false tales of panic and disintegration in the Army of Tennessee. Bragg hoped to lure the methodical Rosecrans into a rash act.

Meanwhile, Bragg's army grew stronger; he was sent reinforcement from Mississippi, where Joe Johnston, as usual, seemed determined to keep them idle on the defensive, and from the forces in east Tennessee driven back by Burnside's march on Knoxville. Bragg's army was built back up to a strength of about 55,000 men, in four corps of two infantry divisions each, a total of 26 infantry brigades. These numbers compared very favorably with the figures of the *Army of the Cumberland*. Rosecrans had little more than 60,000 men in three corps totaling eleven infantry divisions and 33 infantry brigades. But Bragg had a big advantage; for Rosecrans' army was divided as it passed through the mountains, while Bragg's army was concentrated, waiting a little beyond the mountains, ready and able—or so it seemed—to strike the divided Yankees hard and crush them piecemeal.

As always, Bragg's mood swung from day to day. He grew aggressive at the thought that his trap was working, that he was cleverly luring Rosecrans' divided army toward its destruction; then he grew somber, daunted by the memory of past frustrations and the enormity of his present task. He did not really know exactly where Rosecrans' troops were; and in that broken country of thick woods and tall, rugged mountains where movement would be ever so slow, knowing the approximate whereabouts of the foe was certainly not good enough—one had to know exactly, or he would not have time to move rapidly enough to be able to strike hard. Bragg felt as if he were blind. He confessed bitterly to newly arrived Harvey Hill, "It is said to be easy to defend a mountainous country, but the mountains hide your foe from you, while they are full of gaps through which he can

Birdseye view of Chattanooga from Lookout Mountain. Confederates occupied this position when they besieged the Army of the Cumberland after the Battle of Chickamauga. At right: Union engineers lay a pontoon bridge across the Tennessee River below the railroad bridge destroyed by the retreating Confederates. The bridge was later repaired to allow trains to supply the Army of the Cumberland as it pursued Bragg. Below: Victorious Union troops enter Chattanooga after successfully maneuvering Bragg's army out of the city.

pounce upon you at any time. A mountain is like the wall of a house full of rat holes. The rat lies hidden at his hole, ready to pop out when no one is watching. Who can tell what lies hidden behind that wall?"

Nevertheless, strengthened by his reinforcements, Bragg resolved to attack. He decided to use his cavalry to block the forces comprising the northern (Crittenden's *XXI Corps*) and southern (McCook's *XX Corps*) wings of the Union army while concentrating the infantry power of his army, some 40,000 troops, against the isolated center of the Federal army—Thomas' bulky *XIV Corps* of about 23,000 men—and squash it against the mountains; then he would reconcentrate, swing north, and destroy Crittenden's isolated corps.

It was the evening of 9 September, and Braxton Bragg readied the Army of Tennessee to strike hard for the first time in more than eight months.

And as Bragg's army prepared to fight, its hopes were further buoyed by a rumor of more potent aid. Lt. Gen. James Longstreet's corps was supposedly soon to arrive from the Army of Northern Virginia, to at last succor the hard-pressed men of Bragg's Army of Tennessee; and unlike most military rumors of good fortune ahead, this one was actually true. Burly, hard-fighting "Old Peter" and two of his divisions—his third, Pickett's division, was still hard hurt and rebuilding two months past its doomed charge on the last day at Gettysburg—were well and truly moving westward on iron rails.

Longstreet's movement was, at the time, the most rapid movement of large numbers of sol-

diers over a long distance directly to a battlefield in history, a record destined to be eclipsed by the industrious Yankees in a scant few weeks. It was spurred at first, as are many things in history, by a great fear of something that would not come to pass—the fears of the Confederate leadership of a junction in Tennessee of the Union armies of Rosecrans and Burnside, fears stimulated by the fall of Knoxville. The possibility of this Union concentration to crush Bragg worried the Confederate leadership more than the menace of a Federal advance down the Chattanooga-Atlanta rail link to the heartland of the South. Davis and his advisers thus now revived the old plan of achieving a rapid concentration of their own in the West, combining elements of Lee's army with Bragg's newly strengthened army through use of the Confederate advantage of interior lines, and thus obtaining numerical superiority against the *Army of the Cumberland;* if the Confederates could but move fast enough they might be able to crush Rosecrans' army before Burnside's corps could join it, and then turn and destroy Burnside's isolated forces, too, driving the Yankees from Tennessee at long last. This done, the heartland and its precious resources once more secure, the Confederates would be able to shift forces from the center of their extended defensive front to the ends, now better able to contain Grant's army in Mississippi and Meade's in Virginia; the war would revert to stalemate. And each day the independent South survived, its credibility as a nation increased; for the South did not have to conquer to win, but merely to survive.

Of course, past plans to obtain a Confederate concentration in the West had all failed due to the opposition of the Confederacy's greatest soldier, Gen. Robert E. Lee. Lee's outstanding tactical operations—he was certainly the finest battlefield tactician of the Civil War, and arguably the finest high battlefield commander in American military history—in opposition to a numerically superior Union army in the Eastern campaign and his gentle, self-effacing personality gave him enormous status. Lee led by love; men did his bidding because it hurt them so to disappoint him. Yet Lee had a military blind spot. His emotional ties to his native state of Virginia rendered his strategic thought too provincial; to Lee, the Civil War would be won or lost in the ninety-mile stretch of rural, wooded ground between Washington and Richmond, and any significant diversion of force to the West would thus make the war that much harder to win. As long as Lee was successful, so did his logic prosper in the high councils of the Confederacy; but defeat weaned some from his ideas.

It was clear after the disaster at Gettysburg (1–3 July 1863) that it would be a long time before the army of that most aggressive of leaders, Bobby Lee, would be fit to once more take the offensive. And the cautious commander of the Union *Army of the Potomac*, Maj. Gen George Gordon Meade, impressed by the grim lesson of the destruction of his predecessors at the hands of the redoubtable men of Lee, was disinclined immediately to take the offensive. So in the East one commander was unable, and one unwilling, to attack. It was thus a propitious moment for the Confederacy to shift forces to the West.

Lee reluctantly went along with the transfer, but he refused to take command of the new Western concentration in place of Bragg, an end devoutly wished for by President Davis; for not only would such a change put his best field commander in what had suddenly become the decisive theater of operations, it would allow him at last to be rid of the divisive Bragg. But Lee refused; his heart, as ever, belonged to Virginia.

Robert E. Lee, probably the greatest military mind the nation has ever produced, poses on his steed Traveller. Lee dispatched his most brilliant lieutenant James Longstreet to reinforce Bragg in the west.

But "Ol' Pete" Longstreet was enamoured of the idea of the Western concentration; not only did he believe that it made good strategic sense, but it offered him a great personal opportunity. Independent-minded to the point of obstinacy, Longstreet respected Lee, but also envied him; it was hard for a proud, aggressive leader like Longstreet to serve under Lee, a monument of military perfection. Longstreet wanted more recognition of his own fine professional abilities; and he was one of the very few men who did not respond with full deference to Lee's personal system of command through love; at times he strongly disagreed with Lee and even dared to obstruct his commanding officer's designs when he did not deem them worthy. Longstreet needed to stand in the sunshine himself, out from under the shade of the massive shadow of Bobby Lee. Ol' Pete wanted an independent command, and he knew the place to get it was the West. He hoped, and expected, to do well in battle in Tennessee—and then do good for himself, as well. Old Peter Longstreet hungered after Braxton Bragg's command, the Army of Tennessee.

Ready to depart for the West, Longstreet rode one more time to the headquarters of the Army of Northern Virginia to say goodbye to his mentor and emotional rival, the paternal Lee. They talked quietly for a time in Lee's tent. Then it was time for Longstreet to go, and Lee walked him out to his horse. The strapping Georgian put one foot in the stirrup, about to climb up into the saddle, when Lee suddenly spoke. The kindly gray-bearded officer said quietly, "Now, General, you must beat those people out in the West." Longstreet put his foot back down on the ground and turned to face Lee. Mindful of the numerous tactical victories that were causing heavy causalties and hastening the Confederacy down the road of strategic defeat, Longstreet—never a man to shrink from acknowledgment of bitter realities—in a way at once weary and determined said simply, "If I live. But I would not give a single man of my command for a fruitless victory." Unbeknownst to either man, Old Peter Longstreet was not merely summing up the past; he was prophesying the future.

Longstreet's two divisions—under Maj. Gen. Lafayette McLaws and the wounded, worn, but

James Longstreet.

Railroad, nearly doubling the mileage and the time element in the logistical equation. The troops were now routed via southern Virginia, through the Carolinas to Augusta, Georgia, thence northwest to Atlanta and, finally, to Catoosa Station, in north Georgia—an indirect route of 965 miles. Sixteen different railway lines were involved in the transfer of Longstreet's corps, and it was necessary to change trains and unload and then reload equipment numerous times at places where there were no through connections due to lack of contiguous rail links, different track gauges, or unbridged rivers.

The Southern railway system was limited not only in extent, but in equipment, as well. The region lacked the manufacturing capacity to replace worn-out equipment, and was limited in the amount of materials and technical expertise at hand to effect meaningful repairs. Thus, the rolling stock and rails deteriorated from constant use.

The old trains were filled up with the jaunty, gray-clad veteran infantry of the Army of Northern Virginia. Their baggage and equipment was packed and stowed aboard. The artillerymen tugged and pushed wary horses up ramps into boxcars and loaded fodder; then they manhandled the guns and caissons onto flatcars, making them fast with chocks and blocks. The ordnance men loaded ammunition, and the quartermasters rations. And as soon as the motley trains were loaded, they started off.

Thousands of soldiers from the Army of Virginia, such as these below, were dispatched to reinforce their compatriots in the West. The combined Rebel forces at Chickamauga represented one of the few instances when a Southern army actually outnumbered its Union adversary.

ebullient and aggressive Texan, Maj. Gen. John Bell Hood—and the corps artillery began to move out from Orange Court House, Virginia, on 8 September. The Western concentration was a massive logistical project. The Union army's capture of Knoxville denied the Confederacy the use of the direct, 550-mile route from Virginia to north Georgia via the East Tennessee & Virginia

ENTRAINING AND DETRAINING

Logistical Arrangements for the Movement of Troops by Rail

By 1863 the movement of troops by rail had become a sophisticated art, as witnessed by the ambitious Confederate movement of Longstreet's corps from Virginia to the Chattanooga area in September and the even more ambitious Union movement of Hooker's command shortly thereafter.

Infantry Regiment. The infantry was the easiest arm of all to move by rail, making fewest demands on resources. A full regiment of approximately 1,000 men—a rarity in the Civil War—with all their equipment, stores, transport, and animals, required approximately 40 wagons and two or three locomotives.

Rolling Stock Requirement

TYPE OF CAR	NUMBER
Passenger	16–18
Box	5– 7
Flat	6
Horse	12

The figures given are for a comfortable, orderly movement, without crowding the troops. In a pinch, the manpower of the regiment could be crammed into as few as a dozen passenger cars, or, for that matter, into any of the other types of wagon. Similarly, many of the regiment's 200 or so horses and mules, 30 to 50 tons of stores, and most of its wagons could be left behind, so that as few as 20 cars of various types might be required. Fully equipped troops could board a train in a matter of minutes, but it required about 20 minutes to load the animals, wagons, and supplies. Infantry could detrain with great speed and could go into action almost immediately.

Cavalry Battalion. Cavalry was rather difficult to move by rail and required considerable resources. To transport four companies of cavalry—about 420 men plus all their animals, equipment, and impedimenta—by rail required some 40 to 50 cars plus two or three locomotives.

Rolling Stock Requirement

TYPE OF CAR	NUMBER
Passenger	7–8
Box	2–5
Horse	30–40

Unlike the infantry, cavalry could not readily be crowded into fewer wagons. At best, by crowding the men and reducing stores to a minimum, one could reduce the rolling stock requirements by perhaps 20 percent. A battalion of cavalry required about a half hour to entrain. Detraining required about the same amount of time. Cavalry could not always immediately go into action up detraining, particularly if the horses had been long in the cars.

Artillery Battery. Artillery was the most difficult arm to transport by rail, though, of course, its combat power more than compensated for this. A six gun battery required, for its 150 or so men, stores, animals, equipment, and baggage, from 23 to 38 wagons, plus two or three locomotives, depending upon the type of artillery pieces.

Rolling Stock Requirement

TYPE OF CAR	NUMBER
Passenger	3
Box	1
Flat	12–20
Horse	8–15

The rolling stock requirements for the artillery could not be reduced much without unduly complicating loading and unloading, though the troops could ride with the guns and horses, thus eliminating the passenger wagons. Artillery was difficult to load onto a train—at least a half hour for a battery, the time increasing with the caliber of the pieces—and required special equipment to be done with any degree of speed. Detraining was equally difficult and, as with cavalry, the artillery could not always go immediately into action upon detraining.

Longstreet's chief of staff wrote: "Never before were so many troops moved over such worn-out railways, none first-class from the beginning. Never before were such cars—passenger, baggage, mail, coal, box, platform—all and every sort, wobbling on the jumping strap-iron—used for hauling good soldiers."

Longstreet's 12,000 men were in an antic mood. Reprieved for a brief while from the possibility of sudden, violent death, they saw the sojourn as a novel lark, a kind of vacation from battle. And the infantrymen were glad for once to ride, not walk. They tried not to think for a time about what lay ahead in the green, deep, dusky forests of northwest Georgia. And the detour southward, while an evil blow to the Confederate strategists and logisticians, was a boon to the soldiers; the extended route brought many of Longstreet's men through home parts of the Carolinas and Georgia. Smiling, welcoming groups lined the tracks, waving flags and handkerchiefs; the soldiers whooped joyously, basking in their hero's role. And there were ample pretty blushing girls to ogle and call out to appreciatively. Frustrated troops in enclosed freight cars, eager to participate in the celebration of themselves and to have a chance to see the pretty girls or to catch perhaps a fleeting glimpse of family or long-time friends of older, better days, chopped out the sides of the cars in order to see and be seen, seeking instinctively some shining memory to sustain them in the battle growing ever nearer. And so the endless trains chuffed and juddered on.

But not all the passers-by grinned and cheered; some knew enough to also cry. One lady saw a train roll through Kingsville, South Carolina; ". . . I caught a glimpse of Longstreet's Corps going past. God bless the gallant fellows . . . not one rude word did I hear. It was a strange sight. What seemed miles of platform cars, and soldiers rolled in their blankets lying in rows with their heads all covered, fast asleep. In their gray blankets packed in regular order, they looked like swathed mummies. One man . . . was writing on his knee. He used his cap for a desk. . . . I watched him, wondering to whom that letter was to go. To his home, no doubt. Sore hearts for him There!. . . . A feeling of awful depression laid hold of me. All these fine fellows going to kill or be killed, but why?. . . . When a knot of boyish, laughing young creatures passed, a queer feeling of sympathy shook me. Ah, I know how your homefolks feel. Poor children!"

North of Atlanta, congestion was thick on the Western & Atlantic R.R. The worn engines were sometimes only barely able to climb the steep mountain grades. One locomotive was forced to make three running starts before it gained sufficient momentum to pull its train up Allatoona Mountain.

And when the long ride was done, the infantrymen disembarked and, as they always did, walked into battle. John Bell Hood's men left the trains at Ringgold and tramped west, the Third Arkansas Infantry in the lead. After marching a while, the infantrymen came upon

Civil War Rolling Stock

At the time of the Civil War there was great confusion in American railroading. There was no such thing as a standard gauge and depending on terrain and the condition of trackage, Civil War trains averaged 16 to 22 wagons—some 250 to 300 tons—at 15 to 20 miles an hour, though in the Confederacy the average speed was about half this due to track and equipment problems.

As a result, rolling stock from one line might not be able to operate on the tracks of another. Indeed, the capacity of rolling stock from different lines might vary

greatly. Nevertheless, it is possible to get some idea of the capabilities of various types of rolling stock, keeping in mind the considerable degree of variation prevalent at the time.

TYPE OF CAR	Passengers	Cargo Capacity	
		TONS	CUBIC YDS.
Passenger	56		
Box		10–15	50–55
Flat		8–12	15–23
Horse	15–20		

Passenger cars were fitted with seats—sleepers didn't come along

until after the war—and in a pinch could hold 80 men, though some staff officers seemed to think 100 was possible. The critical limitation on the utility of the other types of wagons lay not so much in their tonnage capacity as in their cubic volume: a single 3" rifled cannon with its caisson and pair of limbers weighed considerably less than eight tons, but required more than one flat car for efficient transport.

The better locomotives of the period theoretically could haul some 50 loaded freight wagons "on the flat"—a gross weight of some 800 tons—at 15 miles per hour.

fifty unguarded horses tied to a rail fence; the mounts belonged to a sister outfit, the Third Arkansas Cavalry. The Arkansas infantry thought it but neighborly to be allowed to borrow the horses of their fellow Razorbacks to ease their march forward; and they left in return a sardonic note of thanks:

Tired of long walking and needing a rest,
Your steeds we have gratefully seized and
  impressed,
Feeling it but fair you should do a little walking,
And put yourselves where you can do a lot of
  talking
With the Third Arkansas Infantry, your old friends
  and neighbors,
Who have come from Virginia to share in your
  labors,
And the Lord being willing, the Yankees to
  smite. . . .
We'll camp beyond doubt, after a while,
Though you may have to foot it mile after mile;
But come till you find us—it will give you
  exercise. . . .

And so Ol' Peter's infantry moved up along the narrow dirt roads through the dark, dense forests of northwest Georgia to bring much needed help to their brethren in the command of Bragg.

But the Southern railroad concentration, as remarkable as it was, was not fully successful. The South's railway system was simply not up to so big a task at that stage of the war. Three of Longstreet's infantry brigades and all of the

Patrick R. Cleburne, a hard-fighting Irishman, and one of the greatest Confederate Western commanders. His division distinguished itself at both Chickamauga and Missionary Ridge.

corps artillery, nearly 5,000 men, did not reach northwest Georgia in time to take part in the Battle of Chickamauga. And, indeed, had Ol' Peter had three more of his tried brigades ready to hand on that fateful Sunday, 20 September 1863, he might well have smashed Rosecrans' army, and in the process given the Confederacy one last chance to survive. But as Ol' Peter had wisely told Lee back in Virginia, the Confederacy desperately needed at that moment, not a fruitless, but a decisive, victory. And the depleted Southern railway system was not fully able to achieve the rapid concentration necessary to achieve that decisive victory.

But this was far from the only—and perhaps not even the most important—reason why Confederate arms would fail to gain a significant victory along the west bank of Chickamauga Creek that fateful September Sunday. For as the trains rolled westwards, Bragg struggled to prepare his blow against Rosecrans.

As the Confederate leadership ordained belated succor to him, Braxton Bragg was putting into effect his sound design of concentrating against the center of Rosecrans' dispersed army. Thomas' lead division had emerged from the eastern end of Stevens' Gap into McLemore's Cove, a low valley through which flowed Chickamauga Creek, boxed in to the west by the high, tangled massifs of Missionary Ridge, to the south by the long, curving, jagged spur of high, spiny ground that linked Lookout Mountain and Pigeon Mountain, and to the east by Pigeon Mountain. Thomas' lead division had entered a cul-de-sac, open only at the northern end; it would not break out into open country until, continuing its eastward march, it passed through Dug Gap, between the two massifs of Pigeon Mountain—and there it would find D. H. Hill's corps waiting for it, poised to strike hard before it could fully deploy out of the pass into the open country. But Bragg, wisely, did not intend Hill to wait; for he realized that Rosecrans might at any moment awake to the danger to his army and pull the widespread corps together. If and when that happened, the Army of Tennessee's chance for a great victory would be vastly diminished, if not entirely lost. So Bragg could not wait; he had to strike hard at Thomas' exposed units—fast.

Bragg's plan was a good one. Maj. Gen. Patrick R. Cleburne's division of Hill's corps was assigned to attack due west through Dug Gap to block and pin the Yankee division in the valley of McLemore's Cove. Cleburne was a fighting Irishman, and one of the best tacticians in the

Confederate army, an officer both hard-fighting and wise. Cleburne's move begun, Maj. Gen. Thomas C. Hindman's division of Polk's corps would move south from Lee and Gordon's Mill on the bank of Chickamauga Creek and strike hard into the enemy division's exposed northern flank and rear. Hindman's men were recent transfers from the West to Bragg's army, but they were of proven mettle. Hindman himself was dapper and well seasoned, but his fights in the West had not ended well, and it remained to be seen if he was as capable as he seemed.

Bragg was soon to find that his new leaders were prima donnas. Harvey Hill, while aggressive, was—much like Bragg himself—a punctilious, querulous, contentious subordinate. Bragg's plan was good, but his orders lacked a lawyer's specificity and a teacher's clarity of expression—they tended to be a mite too general, and thus discretionary, in their wording. This left much initiative to subordinates. Unfortunately, because of his well known tendency to blame subordinate commanders when all did not go well with his plans, Bragg had helped to kill the initiative of his corps and division commanders; when in doubt, they did not take action, but tended to wait for more specific instructions from the commanding general which might absolve them of responsibility in the event of tactical defeat. And, of course, battle is full of doubt; so Bragg's commanders had ample reason to do a lot of waiting.

Tom Hindman set out in the first hour of 10 September and made good progress; his division covered nine miles, and by 0600, they were within four miles of the objective. Here Hindman halted. He was worried because he had heard nothing of Harvey Hill. He was fearful of continuing his advance lest the Federal division ahead defeat him before Hill could join him in battle. So he waited.

In the Civil War, command depended primarily upon personal communications, mainly written messages delivered by hand. A lot could go wrong with such a system. The messenger bearing Bragg's orders had found it hard to find Hill in the dark forest. Hill did not set eyes upon Bragg's orders until 0430, and when he finally did so, he most emphatically did not like what he read. Hill had not liked the despondent, self-pitying feel of this strange Western army since joining it; it was not what he was used to, and it made him uncomfortable. And as Hill grew more uncomfortable and distressed in his new surroundings, he also grew unexpectedly timid. Hill believed that Thomas had purposefully ex-

Thomas C. Hindman was blamed by Bragg for the failure to attack Thomas' unsuspecting lead division in McLemore's Cove.

posed his lead Yankee division "as . . . bait" in a clever trap. He wrote Bragg to inform him that his orders could not be obeyed because Pat Cleburne was ill and Hill's other units were otherwise assigned. Bragg swallowed this lame excuse. He decided to send Maj. Gen. Simon Bolivar Buckner's corps to support Hindman's corps in the attack. By 1700, Buckner and his men reached Hindman, who had not advanced his division a foot forward in eleven hours.

Meanwhile, the oblivious Yankee division (the *2nd* of Thomas' *XIV Corps*) of Brig. Gen. James S. Negley continued its march eastward to Dug Gap. Hill immediately deployed the division of the miraculously recovered Pat Cleburne to block the pass from the front and wrote the comatose Hindman, urging him to swing in behind the Yankee division and seal off Dug Gap from the rear. If this were done the Union division would be trapped in the pass, strung out in extended column; the lead division of Thomas' corps could thus be readily destroyed.

Bragg was rigid in temperament. Once he had laboriously decided upon a course of action he was extremely reluctant to alter it or depart from it in any particular. Also, he was ignorant of the locations of many of Thomas' and McCook's units; he wondered if, after all, there might not be other, unknown Union forces in ready supporting distance of McLemore's Cove. Bragg's lack of knowledge rendered him unsure. So he merely forwarded Hill's advice to Hindman for his "information and guidance." He did not order Hindman to follow Hill's wise plan and attack the rear of Negley's vulnerable Yankee

General James S. Negley and his staff. Negley took the lead division of Thomas' Corps into McLemore's Cove and the presence of the Army of Tennessee. Bragg and his subordinates effectively bungled all attempts to crush Negley who retreated to safety.

division at the western end of Dug Gap. Bragg, paradoxically, was as indecisive as he was rigid. When in doubt he left too much initiative and responsibility in the hands of his subordinates, in this case an officer new to the army, whose abilities were unknown and who was unfamiliar with the terrain in which he was operating; and when in doubt, Bragg's subordinate commanders would try to duck that unwanted responsibility.

An hour after Buckner had joined the irresolute Hindman, Bragg rushed a hasty note to the latter, urging him to hurry in his assigned task. Bragg was getting worried, because he had word of Crittenden's *XXI Corps* moving down through Rossville Gap, and he feared that these troops would soon be in position to strike the rear of the units of Buckner and Hindman. But Bragg's staff once again drafted loosely-worded orders. There was no direct order to Hindman to strike at a specific point at a specified time. So Bragg's message failed to impel Hindman forward; indeed, it merely provided him with another reason not to advance—he was reluctant to move further south with Crittenden's men coming down from the north on to his line of retreat.

Hindman spent the night conferring with his staff and Buckner, and then sent off contradictory messages to Bragg, promising at first to attack at daylight, then listing factors that would probably make it impossible to attack, and finally stating that he could not attack.

Meanwhile, Bragg, as if he did not already have too much on his mind, was writhing in the torment of a new trepidation. He was now coming around to Harvey Hill's original belief: Negley's exposed division was merely a feint; the bulk of Thomas' and McCook's men were concentrating to the south, at Alpine, ready to sweep up across the Army of Tennessee' rear. Since Rosecrans had already accomplished a variation of this very thing twice—defeating Bragg in both the Tullahoma and Chattanooga operations—Bragg was very naturally impressed by this possibility.

However, as the night wore on, better information convinced Bragg that his original instincts were sound. At about midnight, he ordered Hindman to attack at daylight. But the wording of Bragg's orders was once again unclear and seemingly discretionary. He ordered Hindman to carry out his—that is, Bragg's—orders at daybreak; but Hindman swore that he understood Bragg's message to be that he should carry out his own plans—that is, Hindman's expressed intention not to attack—at daylight.

On 11 September, Hindman's and Buckner's units moved forward timidly—progressing a full mile and a half. But Hindman's heart was not in this too uncertain job. He worried about what was in front of him; he worried about his rear. In the late afternoon, after futile consultation with his staff, he decided to retreat. Then he learned from scouts that Negley's division, at last alerted to its peril in the face of three times its number, was rapidly falling back across McLemore's Cove in retreat toward Stevens' Gap and the support of Thomas' other divisions. At that point, 1700 hours on the 11th, after having wasted two full days, Hindman finally advanced toward Dug Gap.

Pat Cleburne and his men had spent the 11th poised in front of Dug Gap, ready to attack—as per Bragg's orders—as soon as they heard the rumble of Hindman's artillery firing at the other end of the pass. But they never heard those guns until nearly sunset. And when they advanced into the pass, they found no Yankees; and in McLemore's Cove they found only Hindman's lead units.

It was a fiasco born of the increasing paralysis of command and control in the Army of Tennessee. No one any longer had any confidence in Bragg's judgments and orders; his field commanders—Hill, Hindman, Buckner—all thought that they were wiser and knew better than their chief. Bragg's leading officers no longer considered his orders binding.

Bragg himself blamed Hindman's excessive timidity for the debacle; but his own uncertainty, shifts of mind and mood, and his unwillingness—lest he be proved wrong—to firmly and decisively commit his divisions to the assault in McLemore's Cove also played a large role in this astounding failure of command in battle. But no one yet perceived the larger and more ominous problem: the chain of command of the Army of Tennessee was in the process of disintegration.

Bragg resolved to try again to carry out his intention to destroy the leading units of one of Rosecrans' isolated corps; and another such shining opportunity quickly presented itself. But the results would be the same. And so would be the reason for failure.

Federal Maj. Gen. Tom Crittenden, a bluff, hearty Regular, had sent two of his XXI Corps divisions on toward Ringgold, and hooked one division south down along Chickamauga Creek

toward Lee and Gordon's Mills. Bragg intended that Bishop Polk's corps, supported by the reserve corps under command of Brig. Gen. William H. T. Walker, should strike Crittenden's isolated division at daybreak on the 13th and destroy it; then the four Confederate divisions should drive north, cut the road to Ringgold behind Crittenden's other two divisions, and destroy them, too. As Bragg optimistically told Polk, "This division crushed and the others are yours." To make sure that there would be no misunderstanding of orders this time, Bragg issued a direct order to Polk at 2000 hours, 12 September, to attack the isolated Yankee division at daylight the next morning.

But Bragg's well conceived plan was soon aborted. While Ben Cheatham's division moved with reasonable promptness on the 12th to get into position for the next day's attack, Tom Hindman once again delayed too long. Hindman had been ordered to join Cheatham in position to attack by the afternoon of the 12th, moving as soon as his troops were "refreshed" from their dubious exertions of past days. But Hindman indulgently gave his men too long a rest. He and his men did not report to Polk until 0430 on 13 September—about an hour before they were scheduled to attack! But Hindman need not have worried. The attack was not going to take place, after all.

Crittenden, like Thomas before him, had belatedly awoken to the mortal peril to his corps, and had moved rapidly to reunite his three divisions. Polk's reconnaissance troops detected this reconcentration, and the Bishop reasoned that Bragg's original orders were no longer valid in the changed circumstances; Polk decided not to attack, informing Bragg of this late on the night of the 12th, and demanding reinforcements.

Bragg insisted that Polk go ahead with the attack, pointing out that he still had four divisions to throw against Crittenden's three. Bragg also promised to send Buckner's two divisions up to support Polk; this was too good an opportunity to let pass by. He reassured Polk that contrary to his fears, Crittenden was not being reinforced; Thomas and McCook were still far distant. Bragg's latest order was well reasoned, but somewhat rambling and a little vague in its wording; he expressed his hope and preference that Polk would attack, but did not directly tell him to do so. It was almost as if Bragg subconsciously did not himself want the attack to go forward; what his mind consciously directed, his subconscious countermanded through lack of clarity and focus in his written orders. Per-

Alexander McCook, commander of the XX Corps of the Army of the Cumberland. He defeated the right wing of the Union lines at Chickamauga.

haps this confusion was merely an outward manifestation of Bragg's emotional insecurity, which rendered him both rigid and indecisive.

In any event, with these new, more flexible orders to justify his decision, Polk resolved not to attack.

On the morning of the 13th, all was quiet in the woods. Bragg heard no sound of artillery thunder. He and his staff went forward to confer with Polk, riding ahead of Buckner's lead division, going to succor the reluctant Bishop. When Bragg arrived at Polk's headquarters, at about 0900, he discovered that Polk had not yet deployed his divisions in position for the assault; Polk was concerned only with defending his own lines, rather than attacking those of the enemy, and he had pulled his units back to form a long, semicircular defensive front. Angrily Bragg seethed, while Polk repositioned his troops and conducted another reconnaissance; not until the afternoon did the bulk of Polk's and Walker's men begin to move slowly forward. But it was, once again, too late. Crittenden's units had fallen back across to the west bank of Chickamauga Creek the previous night. So both Bragg's urgency to attack and Polk's fear to attack had been in vain; by the morning of the 13th, there was no one to attack.

Bragg was bitter and frustrated. The command structure of his army was disintegrating. His subordinates mistrusted his judgment and his tactics; so they doubted his orders, and believed themselves wise and right in not considering them binding nor seriously trying to execute them. In his turn, Bragg had completely lost faith in his subordinate commanders. He knew that they had repeatedly failed him, and so he could not and did not trust them. Bragg sank into depression and self-pity, grieving over lost opportunities that were not yet gone.

Bragg's instincts had been sound thus far, his plans well-founded. He had failed because he made the amateurish error of confusing orders issued with orders executed. Bragg was a dismal follow-up general. Once he had decided what he wanted to do, and issued orders to get it done, he fatalistically stepped out of the command structure and allowed events to develop a momentum of their own without trying to influence them; he should have used his staff to exercise much more direct supervision over his corps and division commanders to ensure the prompt effecting of his orders. That he did not do so was partly habit. It was easy to control the small units of the peacetime frontier army without recourse to large, efficient staffs; staff officers had no practical experience in knitting the command and control structure of the big, sprawling Civil War armies. Staff officers—like field officers—were left to learn by doing; and some learned faster and better than others. Where a commander had a strong and decisive personality that inspired confidence in those around him—as in the case of Grant—or when a commander was blessed with an able subordinate whose initiative could invariably be relied on—a relationship that Lee enjoyed with Jackson—it was possible to temper the inadequacies of the flawed system. In the Army of Tennessee this was not possible. Bragg was a cold, sullen loner who lacked the warmth and compassion to win the affections of men and thus build a loving, supportive, close-knit staff; his failures in battle inspired mistrust, not confidence, in his tactical commanders. And his subordinates were not men of great ability, and were utterly lacking in initiative.

The other problem in this chaos of command and control was Bragg's emotional insecurity. Did he really want to attack? Rationally, he did. But subconsciously perhaps he did not. His rigid personality demanded perfection. Battles are not gems of perfection; they are messy and chaotic, fundamentally often as uncontrollable as a natural disaster. To a man of Bragg's ordered, systematic, structured temperament, fluidity and disorder—the very prerequisites of battle—were daunting. Hence, his desire as a tactician to establish a plan at the outset and then to try to cling to it throughout the duration of a battle, like a desperate survivor to a piece of wreckage, no matter what changes occurred in the tactical situation; the outward reality was much less important than the inner peace derived from a fixed, inflexible course of action. Also, to engage in battle was necessarily to risk defeat, which to the punctilious Bragg, meant sustaining insupportable humiliation. This is why when he fought and failed to win he blamed defeat on others. A painless way to avoid defeat was to avoid battle. So outwardly in this period Bragg was aggressive, anxious to bring on a battle; yet the written and physical signals he sent out to his subordinate commanders—vague orders, lack of direct staff supervision of their performance—were indecisive. Bragg was a paradox of rigidity and indecisiveness, and this undermined his ability to command and control his army.

And, most likely, all of this made scant difference, for the basic trouble, as the leading historian of the Army of Tennessee has written, was that Bragg's army was "at an impasse, with Bragg no longer trusting his officers to independent operations, while they both feared such responsibility and at the same time mistrusted his direct orders as being potentially disastrous."

In any event, morose and bitterly disappointed, Bragg lapsed into a torpor of disgruntled pessimism. Nevertheless, he should have persisted. The objective situation had not changed all that much. Crittenden was five miles away, across Chickamauga Creek; Thomas was more than ten miles from Crittenden, down in McLemore's Cove; and McCook was still far to the south, more than thirty miles distant. Bragg could still strike hard with his entire force at Crittenden; and even in the unlikely event that Thomas could have gotten up fast enough to support Crittenden in strength, Bragg's army would still only be fighting two-thirds of Rosecrans' army with all of his own. But Bragg had no more heart for a fight.

Thomas L. Crittenden, leader of the XXI Corps of the Army of the Cumberland. Isolated from the rest of the Union forces, he was in danger of being crushed by Bragg's entire army. Once again the Confederate operation was bungled and an opportunity for victory lost. **Below:** *General Alexander McCook's headquarters in Stevenson, Alabama. In pursuing Bragg after taking Chattanooga, the Army of the Cumberland became dangerously overextended. McCook's XX Corps was several days marching distance from the rest of the army. Meanwhile, Bragg unsuccessfully attempted to wipe out the divided Union corps.*

Bragg was not completely sure exactly where all of Crittenden's and Thomas' divisions—much less McCook's—were. Once again he felt like a blind man. This was partly due to the nature of the impenetrable terrain of northwest Georgia, dense woodlands and steep, jumbled mountains, which hindered reconnaissance. But it was also due to the besetting, fatal sin of the Confederate cavalry throughout the Civil War: the romantic preference of its self-centered leaders for dashing, glorious offensive raids rather than the dull, anonymous staple of reconnaissance patrols. Bragg began to wonder again if he were hunting Rosecrans or if Rosecrans was subtly stalking him. He had no idea when all of Longstreet's men would reach him; and his troops were growing short of rations. He feared that Rosecrans was being reinforced by units from Grant's army; and he expected Burnside's troops to hasten from eastern Tennessee to Chattanooga in support of Rosecrans. Despondently, Bragg decided to move his army back to LaFayette.

Thus, while Rosecrans, realizing that his foe was not cowed and in flight, and learning that Bragg had been and was continuing to be reinforced from the West and from Virginia, became duly frightened and sought to bring about the reconcentration of his divided army by much hard marching, Bragg sulked, trying to rationalize his army's failures and come to terms with his bitter grief. Then, on 15 September, looking worn and emaciated, he called together Polk, Hill, Walker, and Buckner for a command conference. The army's leaders agreed that their best plan was to try to outflank Rosecrans' army on the north, to try to get between it and Chattanooga, and then drive it southward in retreat, away from Chattanooga and also away from the possibility of help from Burnside.

Once again, Bragg's instincts were correct, his main concept wise; but, once again he would bungle in the execution of his grand design. First, he wasted time, a full day; the army was not ordered to move forward until the morning of the 17th. Then, too, Bragg never grasped the connection between terrain and tactics. In order to cut Rosecrans' *Army of the Cumberland* off from Chattanooga, it was necessary for the Army of Tennessee to advance boldly upon the northern bridges crossing Chickamauga Creek, drive hard to cut the LaFayette Road—the main north-south route in the valley of the Chickamauga—and then strike all the way to Rossville Gap. Bragg, instead, simply ordered his army forward to deploy his infantry defensively along the east bank of the Chickamauga; he did order his cavalry to seize and hold four crossings—two bridges and two fords—but he completely ignored the two northernmost bridges—Ringgold Bridge and Dyer's Bridge—that led directly to Rossville. Bragg believed that Rosecrans'

Column of Union soldiers, complete with band, prepare to march. After Rosecrans learned of the incredible danger his divided army was in, he desperately tried to reunite the three corps. Union troops marched day and night to avoid catastrophe.

army was deployed on a front from McLemore's Cove, in the south, to Lee and Gordon's Mills, in the north; hence, he now moved his own infantry even further south than before. Then he changed his plan again, moving his units somewhat further north to be sure of overlapping Rosecrans' left flank. But Bragg's northernmost crossing point was to be at Alexander's Bridge, only about four miles north of Lee and Gordon's Mills, but six to ten miles from the two unnoticed but vital northernmost bridges.

Bragg planned to send Walker's division across Alexander's Bridge and Buckner's corps, further south, across at Thedford's Ford, these three divisions to sweep down on Crittenden's corps from the north. Polk's corps was to feint across from Lee and Gordon's Mills to fix Crittenden in place, then force a crossing and attack Crittenden's units frontally while they were also being hard hit in flank by Walker's and Buckner's men. Hill's corps, to the south, would shield the main assault, prepared to strike hard at any of Thomas' units sent north to help Crittenden.

But at last, at this point Bragg began to realize the one great flaw in his otherwise astute plan: his army was deployed too far south to realistically be sure of cutting the Union army off from Rossville. So he had to develop a new plan, consuming yet another day, to shift his army's crossing points to the north, assigning Brig. Gen. Bushrod Johnson's division to assault Reed's Bridge, seven miles northeast of Lee and Gordon's Mills; this was better, but the two northernmost bridges across the Chickamauga were still ignored by Bragg and his staff. The rest of the plan remained basically the same. Bragg, recalling his bitter frustration of a week past, wrote at the end of his field order: "The above movements will be executed with the utmost promptness, vigor, and persistence."

But, while all of this planning was going on, Bragg did not move his army forward to get into position for the continually changing attack; as a result, everybody had to move out at once, on the 18th, and the result was confusion. Walker's men and Buckner's men got jammed up on the road north; Bushrod Johnson's men marched and waited, marched and waited, retracing their steps in a spree of contradictory orders. And the Yankees promptly added to the confusion.

Yankee cavalry held Reed's Bridge, and Johnson had to summon Rebel troopers to drive them back; but the blueclad horse soldiers clung grimly to the western end of the ramshackle, narrow wooden bridge for over three hours, building up, as they always did, a huge volume of fire with their repeating carbines. It was near 1600 hours before Johnson was able to push his units across to the west bank of the Chickamauga, in improved, but not great, positions for the big attack the next day.

At Alexander's Bridge, Walker's men found no bridge; the Union cavalry troopers had ripped out the bridge flooring. Walker had no intention of trying to force the creek. Although flowing sluggishly—deceptively calm—the Chickamauga was deep with steep banks; and the men on the other side seemed to be backed up by artillery and most certainly had the Yankee cavalrymen's ubiquitous rapid-firing carbines. Walker's men retraced their line of march and headed a mile and a half north, crossing the Chickamauga at Bryam's Ford. It was already twilight when Walker's infantrymen waded the chill waters of the winding creek and spread out into the dense thickets on the west bank.

Buckner's units made no attempt to cross the creek at all. Arriving at Thedford's Ford by 1400, Buckner was worried about hearing nothing from the departed Walker. He decided to wait on the east bank. He waited all day.

Thus, on the even of battle, Bragg had only two small divisions, less than twenty percent of his forces, deployed on the west bank of Chickamauga Creek, at what was presumably the critical point, Crittenden's left flank. Bragg was weakest at precisely the point he needed to be strongest. Worse, the troops on the west bank had no idea what they were supposed to do. Bragg's orders had completely omitted the key concept of his plans, the vital necessity of seizing the Union army's line of retreat north and west toward Chattanooga by deploying westward toward the LaFayette Road and northward toward the Rossville Gap. His combat leaders did not even seem to realize that they were to try to turn Crittenden's northern flank once they crossed the creek; that they were to move west before they struck south. Thus, even the units that managed to cross Chickamauga Creek on the 18th were in poor position to achieve the best results when they attacked the following day.

Indeed, after wading the creek, Walker's men simply deployed not far from Alexander's Bridge; they knew that they were supposed to cross the Chickamauga at about that point, but they did not know what they were supposed to do when they got to the other side. Johnson's befuddled men had presumably crossed the creek well north of Crittenden's left flank; yet so ignorant were they of their proper role in the operation that they threw away this tactical advantage by simply marching south from Reed's Bridge, directly across the front of Walker's men!

When lanky, aggressive John B. Hood reached the west bank to take charge of Johnson's motley, confused division, he and W. H. T. Walker conferred, sitting on a log, about what they should do next. Finally, during the early morning, Buckner's units crossed the Chickamauga; and then so did one of Polk's divisions. Only Hill's two divisions and the ever-late Hindman's division were still on the east bank by noon of 19 September. The Army of Tennessee was at last ready to attack; but too much valuable time had been wasted in the process of moving it into position, and even at that late hour, none of Bragg's commanders were sure what their chief wanted them to do.

Thus, Bragg's own indecisiveness and the lack of an efficient staff system in his army produced slackness and loss of command and control in the Army of Tennessee even when he and his subordinates were in basic unity and trying to work toward a common purpose. The Army of Tennessee was weakest at precisely the point that it hoped and needed to be strongest, at the

north flank of the Union lines. But there was worse news ahead for Bragg and his troops, for the *Army of the Cumberland* was not at all where Bragg and his Army of Tennessee thought it was.

While Bragg was planning his battle, Rosecrans was frantically trying to pull the separate strands of his army together, greatly abetted by the delays imposed on the Confederates by the slackness of their command system. He held Crittenden's *XXI Corps* near Lee and Gordon's Mills, and moved Thomas' strong *XIV Corps* north from Stevens' Gap half the way up to Crittenden, to Pond Spring. He also ordered McCook's *XX Corps* north; McCook chose to follow the longest route, but also the one with the best roads, backtracking to the rear of Lookout Mountain, and thence on to Stevens' Gap. And—as it was to turn out, very significantly—Rosecrans moved Gordon Granger's small *Reserve Corps* of one division up from Stevenson all the way to crucial Rossville. As a result of much hard marching by McCook's men, by nightfall on the 17th, Rosecrans' major units were all within about five or six miles of each other, deployed a little east of Missionary Ridge, and a little west of the deep blue, sinuous, sluggish Chickamauga Creek.

Rosecrans felt a little better as he began to get his army in hand once again; yet he had no idea what the Rebels were up to, but their movements were ominous, and the uncertainty troubled him. He was spooked. He screamed unavailingly for succor from Burnside. Then his patrols reported large numbers of Rebels in motion in the woods across the creek. Rosecrans was worried about his open flank to the north, which was also Burnside's route toward him, and his main line of supply and communications stretching back, thin and exposed, toward Chattanooga. Thus, restless and vaguely wary, Rosecrans decided that very night to shift his army further north. He wisely moved Crittenden's corps north from Lee and Gordon's Mills to protect the vital LaFayette Road; he moved Thomas' corps north up to Crawfish Springs, a little southwest of Lee and Gordon's Mills; and he brought McCook's corps up to Pond Spring. As a result of this night marching, Rosecrans' major units were much more tightly concentrated, each now within two or three miles of each other; moreover, Crittenden's corps was now two miles north of where it had been before, unbeknownst to the Confederates. Bragg's plan was already outdated a full day and a half before the battle.

Lee and Gordon's Mills served as a critical position on the Federal right wing under McCook. During the battle Rosecran's headquarters was two miles north of this.

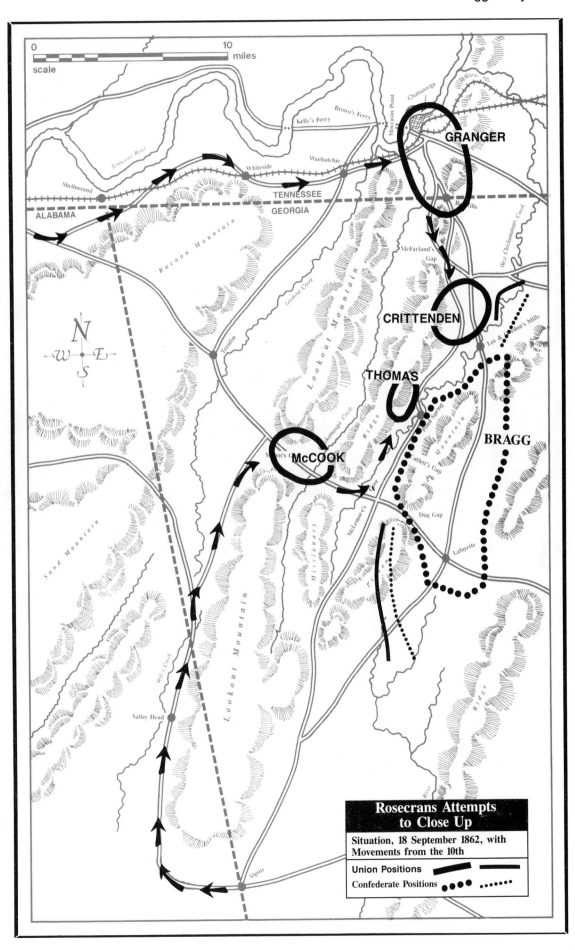

Rosecrans Attempts
to Close Up

Situation, 18 September 1862, with
Movements from the 10th

Union Positions

Confederate Positions

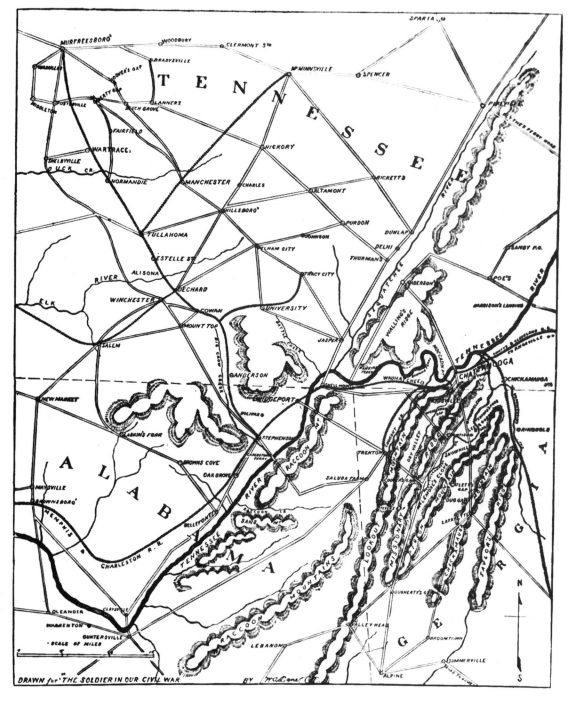

Area of action during the Chicka-mauga Campaign.

Rosecrans made another similarly sage move on 18 September. Still uncomfortable about his left, Rosecrans ordered McCook's corps to move up to Crawfish Springs, releasing Thomas' corps to move in the darkness across the rear of Crittenden's units, which continued to move north. By the morning of the 19th, the Union left had been extended a further two miles north. Thus, the left flank of Rosecrans' army was now fully four miles north of where Bragg and the Confederates thought it to be. And, ironically, Rosecrans' army was now more tightly concentrated than Bragg's army.

Thomas had two divisions installed at a pivotal point. While Negley's division was still at

Crawfish Springs, set to move north, and the division of hard-fighting Maj. Gen. Joseph J. Reynolds was also on the march northward to join its brethren, Thomas had the divisions of Brig. Gen. Absalom Baird and Brig. Gen. John M. Brannan disposed to block the road leading west from Reed's Bridge at its intersection with the key north-south LaFayette Road. Thus, although Bragg's plan was based on turning the Union left, in fact, the Union left extended northward well beyond the Confederate right.

So Rosecrans' army, despite its recent perils, was now in good shape. It could commence battle well positioned and with the early fire-power advantage of the defensive; its units had operated together for a long time, while many units in the foe's army were new to it; and it was under tighter command and control than its opposition. Yet this would not be the kind of battle suited to Rosecrans' thoughtful, methodical temperament. Old Rosy needed time—lots and lots of time—to think and plan. This battle had come upon him unexpected, and he would have little time to think. And so he would never be able really to get a grip on this battle; it would drift on elusively, always just a little beyond his control. Without a plan, and time to think, he would not know what to do; and not knowing what to do, he would do what he had done at the great indecisive bloodletting at Murfreesboro—he would hold on. His sole design was to hold on. But, as at Murfreesboro, this would cost him the initiative in the battle. As long as he still fought Bragg, this failing did not matter. But Old Peter Longstreet was coming, and unlike Braxton Bragg, Longstreet would know exactly what to do to a foe who conceded the initiative. The Battle of Chickamauga would not at all be the kind of fight that Old Rosy would feel comfortable with and do well in. Thus, on the night of 18–19 September, both the Union and Confederate armies were poised for battle, but neither was fully ready.

Crawfish Springs was typical terrain of the Battle of Chickamauga. McCook's forces concentrated here the night before the battle. Richard W. Johnson's First Division of the XX Corps marched five miles from this position to reinforce Thomas.

LOGISTICS AND STRATEGY IN THE

During the Civil War, machine technology—the outset of the industrialization of warfare—enabled both sides to raise and equip much larger field armies than in the past, and railroads allowed the deployment of these armies with unprecedented rapidity. Indeed, the railroads of the North—more numerous and in far better condition than their Southern counterparts—are justly famous for the significant role they played in the victory of the Union. This was so because the North's preponderance of railroads enabled the Union armies to overcome one of the few genuine military advantages enjoyed by the Confederacy in the Civil War—interior lines.

The wiser, less provincial of the Confederate strategists—for example, Davis, despite his rigidity and a variety of other military flaws, was, after all, a Westerner and, thus, in many ways better equipped to formulate a successful strategy for the South than his smarter but narrower Virginia generals—well understood this advantage. They sought to compensate for the Confederacy's comparative lack of numbers by using the interior lines of supply and communication of the more compact South to shift armies rapidly from front to front to concentrate superior forces at a single point and thus defeat piecemeal a foe much larger in overall numbers, who was spread out over greater distances. This was the basis of the Napoleonic strategic thought that the leaders of both armies had absorbed in varying degrees at West Point. Inferior forces were able to take the offensive—and win—against superior numbers by concentrating greater strength against a smaller part of the enemy's overall greater force. This had worked so well for Napoleon because of the unprecedented mobility of the

French army versus its much more slower moving—and thus also much more slower thinking—opponents. However, where the contending armies appeared to be of roughly similar mobility, as in the American Civil War, another way was needed to effect the rapid concentrations of force necessary to achieve victory. That way was the use of interior lines.

The classic example of this is the Chickamauga Campaign. The Confederate leaders sought to use interior lines to concentrate superior forces against the inferior Union army in Tennessee and smash it before it could receive assistance. They did in fact achieve such a concentration; but the inadequacies of the Southern rail net prevented the concentration from being as overwhelming as it might have been, and atrocious command and control arrangements in Bragg's army—as well as the stout hearts and cool brains of men like Pap Thomas and Gordon Granger and their tough, relentless Westerners—ruined the Confederate opportunity. Yet as a result of Chickamauga the Rebels held the high ground around Chattanooga, potentially one of the strongest defense positions in America. Despite this, their rattled leadership lacked the cohesion to utilize this potential. And then the Northern railroads brought to Tennessee a

Union counter-concentration, one strong enough to drive the Confederates from the high ground and open up the Gateway of the South to Yankee invasion. So in the Campaign of Chickamauga the Union rail net ultimately negated the Confederate advantage of interior lines.

It is well to recall that in areas devoid of extensive river systems, the large field armies of the Civil War could not move without assured rail supply lines. Even good roads, which were then relatively rare in rural America, could not sustain the large Civil War armies very far from rail or water transportation. For example, during its advance down across northern Georgia to Atlanta, Billy Sherman's army was supplied by a single-track railroad that delivered to it 160 box cars of provisions and supplies each day. The army's operations took place in a region utterly devoid of good roads—but even had it been deployed in an area with a good road net, it would have required an impossible 220,800 animals and 36,800 wagons to deliver an equivalent amount of supplies! As Sherman wrote, "Therefore . . . the Atlanta campaign was an impossibility without . . . railroads. . . ."

The great bottleneck in the supply system was the need for massive amounts of fodder to feed

WEST IN THE CIVIL WAR

the armies' draft animals and artillery horses; for the men, with their smaller appetites, could be fed at considerable distances from railheads, but the animals could not, as they consumed five to ten times the amount of food as the men. As Pap Thomas ruefully observed of his campaigns in the rough country of Tennessee and north Georgia, "To procure forage it is necessary to send for it 15 miles, and the roads were so difficult that by the time the wagons reach here the wagons have nearly consumed their loads." During the course of the war, Sherman's men—famed for traveling light—had to triple their allocation of supply wagons.

While feeding the armies' animals was the major supply nightmare, it should not be thought that it was a simple matter to feed the men. The South was comparatively sparsely populated and much of its land was not devoted to raising food crops but rather to the production of raw material crops such as cotton, hemp, and tobacco. Further, it has been estimated that about half of the rations supplied to the Union troops in the Civil War were completely wasted due to improper storage, troop carelessness, or improper preparation.

To comprehend the scale of the Union war effort, it is only necessary to note that Army quartermasters consumed over half the total output of Northern industry, mostly in procuring uniforms, tents, shoes, wagons, rations, and so forth. Indeed, in 1861, 270,000 hogs were slaughtered annually in Chicago; at war's end, the number was 900,000 annually.

There is an old soldier's adage that the amateur warrior studies tactics, but the professional warrior studies logistics. The American Civil War in the West—whose outcome hinged on logistics—is a classic example of why this is so. The leaders of both the Union and the Confederacy formulated intelligent strategies based on the principle of concentration, using interior lines for increased mobility. Because Union naval forces were able to control most of the major river systems of the interior and the Northern railroad system was superior to that of the South, the Federal generals were better able to sustain the large-scale offensive concentrations needed to obtain victory than were their Confederate opponents.

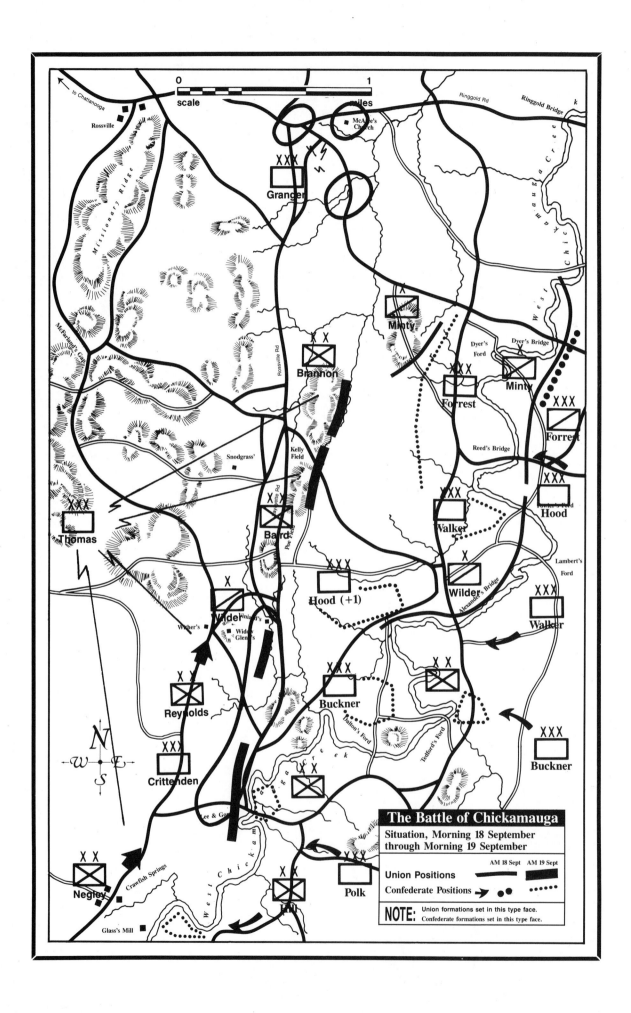

CHAPTER VII

The Battle of Chickamauga

Situation, Morning 18 September
through Morning 19 September

Union Positions
Confederate Positions

AM 18 Sept   AM 19 Sept

NOTE: Union formations set in this type face.
Confederate formations set in this type face.

THE BATTLE OF CHICKAMAUGA, 19–20 SEPTEMBER 1863

Chickamauga—"dwelling place," in the language of the Creek Indians; "river of death," to the first white settlers of that dark woodland valley. An eloquent historian wrote of it: "Chickamauga Creek . . . sinuously wound its way between the armies. . . . Now the character of its quiet flow through the Georgia countryside appeared to alter abruptly like . . . a lake at the approach of a storm. Pallid moonlight on its surface and the eerie mist that rose from it at dawn cast a spell in the minds of men. Its ripples seemed to whisper . . . River of Death. Soldiers who heard that whisper were seized by a strong presentiment that they would not survive the battle. . . . Most of them, striving vainly or successfully to brush that premonition aside, never voiced it. A few confided it to a diary or a comrade. . . . Dark forests, covering the battleground . . . wore a still more ominous aspect. Here and there depths were opened for cabins. Elsehwere light filtered faintly through the shrouding branches . . . murky moonbeams glimmered on a stagnant pool. . . . Neither song of bird nor chirp of cricket sounded in those gloomy shades. They swallowed the armies."

The First Day, 19 September 1863

The Battle of Chickamauga began in an unexpected way on the cool morning of 19 September 1863. The Confederates deployed at the northern end of Bragg's front, on the west bank of the Chickamauga were still milling about uncertainly, unsure what they were supposed to do or when. At sunup, a Union officer had reported erroneously that the Rebels on the west side of the creek at Reed's Bridge were not present in strength; he estimated that only a single brigade was across. George Thomas, usually very careful in the attack, was weary of all the marching and counter-marching and the confusion of the eccentric but ominous movements of the enemy; here now loomed a certainty, and a chance at last to do something meaningful. Thomas decided to crush this apparently isolated Confederate brigade before it could be reinforced; he sent two brigades of John Brannan's division out to do it. When these came up against heavy fire, he quickly sent forward the rest of Brannan's units.

Confederate cavalry troopers saw Brannan's throng coming toward them and deployed on foot, opening fire with carbines and light artillery to delay the Yankee infantry until help could arrive. It is said that the first shots frightened an owl, who broke cover, only to be attacked by several crows. "What a country!" a Tennessee infantryman said. "Even the birds . . . fight!" Even Harvey Hill, who like most infantrymen of his time had no use for cavalry,

Union troops

and who had said that in Virginia he had never seen a dead soldier wearing spurs, lauded the gray horse soldiers and gunners this day. The startled W. H. T. Walker, hearing the sounds of gunfire coming from his vulnerable right rear, left his breakfast and ordered Brig. Gen. States Rights Gist to take his division to the sounds of battle and intervene in the fight.

Gist's gray infantry came swarming out of the brush at Brannan's disconcerted bluecoats. Sent to attack a lone brigade, Brannan's troops now faced the sudden onslaught of a Confederate division; they were not ready for this. One of Brannan's brigade commanders quickly sent back a hasty, caustic message, inquiring which of the many enemy brigades at its front was the one his men had been sent out to take. Gist's men came on, firing, and the blueclad infantry were sent reeling backwards.

Seeing that the developing battle bore a different aspect than he had thought, Thomas ordered Brig. Gen. Absolam Baird's division to the support of Brannan's men. The fire of Baird's troops halted the Rebels for a moment and gave Brannan a chance to get his units in hand again.

But Walker was also willing to up the ante in this encounter battle. He ordered the division of Brig. Gen. St. John Liddell to deploy alongside Gist's men.

The fight soon became a formless struggle of tenacious brigades firing at each other from the brush and trees, each side trying to build up fire superiority for a decisive charge. But the Confederates had an edge; their cavalry troopers overlapped the left flank of the blue infantry,

and their fire tore at the northernmost Yankee units in conjunction with that of Gist's men. The Federal line began to bend, then, under increasing pressure at this weak point, at last to break. The advancing Confederates charged ahead, and the Union troops were driven back, all the way to their original positions a mile east of the vital LaFayette Road. But Baird's and Brannan's men still looked shaky after their unexpected drubbing, and doubting that they could hold there, Thomas asked Rosecrans for reinforcements.

Old Rosy knew that George Henry Thomas was as strong and tough a defensive fighter as the Union Army mustered; if Thomas said he needed help, he did. Besides, Rosecrans had been troubled about his left flank for days. So he decided to send Brig. Gen. John M. Palmer's *2nd Division* of Crittenden's *XXI Corps* and Brig. Gen. Richard W. Johnson's *2nd Division* of McCook's *XX Corps* to the support of Thomas' hard-pressed soldiers.

Johnson's men came up fast and hit hard at Liddell's flank units. Their rapid, heavy fire stopped the Rebels' advance. Once more the lines of Gray and Blue brigades ripped at each other with fire. Then Palmer's men came up, and the Federal infantry began to generate fire superiority. The Rebel lines staggered; the grayclad infantrymen began to fall back. Walker sent up two brigades of Ben Cheatham's hard-fighting division, and they helped the Gray infantry to hold firm.

In the dense woods, with visibility limited, the lines of battle shredded and units lost con-

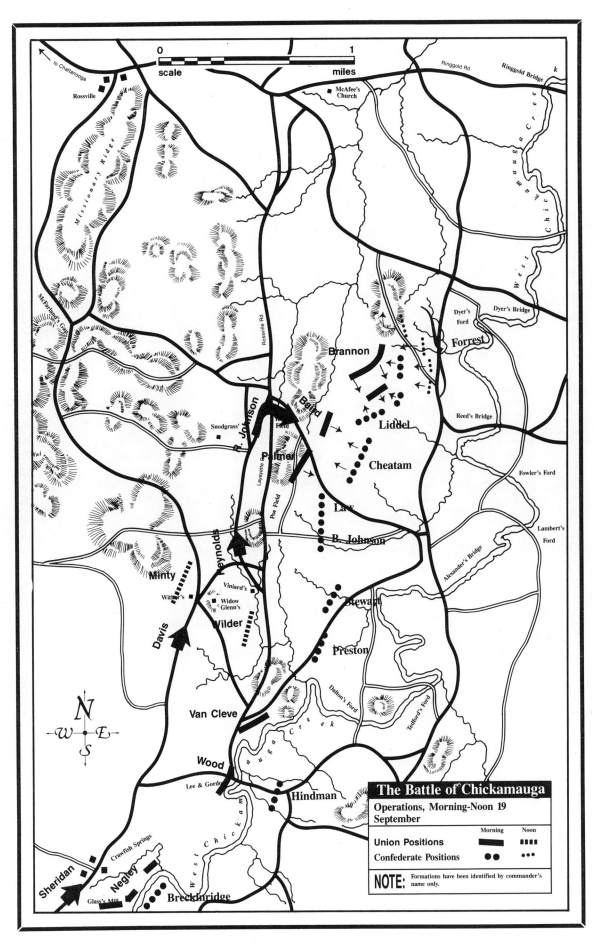

0   scale   1
miles

to Chattanooga

Rossville

Ringgold Rd   Ringgold Bridge   k

McAfee's Church

Missionary Ridge

McFarland's Gap

Dyer's Ford   Dyer's Bridge

Forrest

Brannon

Baird

Snodgrass'

R. Johnson

Field

Palmer

Poe Field

Lafayette Rd

Rossville Rd

Reed's Bridge

Liddel

Cheatam

West Chickamauga Creek

Fowler's Ford

Law

B. Johnson

Lambert's Ford

Alexander's Bridge

Reynolds

Minty

Wither's

Viniard's

Widow Glenn's

Wilder

Stewart

Davis

Preston

Dalton's Ford

Tedford's Ford

Van Cleve

Chickamauga Creek

Wood

Lee & Gordon

Hindman

The Battle of Chickamauga

Operations, Morning-Noon 19 September

	Morning	Noon
Union Positions		
Confederate Positions		

NOTE: Formations have been identified by commander's name only.

Crawfish Springs

Sheridan

Negley

Glass's Mill

West Chickamauga Creek

Breckinridge

N
W · E
S

tact with other outfits ostensibly on their flanks. "The woods loomed," as one historian wrote, "to mask . . . fire. . . . Spurts of red flame from muzzles were the only beacon. . . . The . . . battle ebbed and flowed in sudden, bloody freshets. . . ." The men fought with lonely, desperate fury in the smoky green gloom. An Alabama infantryman described the bitter, almost personal, intensity of the fight as "one solid, unbroken wave of awe-inspiring sound . . . as if all the fires of earth and hell had been turned loose. . . ." In those conditions, as an Indiana infantry officer noted, there could be "no generalship in it. It was a soldier's fight purely. . . . the only question involved was the question of endurance. The . . . armies came together like two wild beasts, and each fought as long as it could stand up. . . ."

The shaken, jagged lines of Blue and Gray infantry stood up in the dappled gray-green-brown woods, sweating and sooty-faced, and fired furiously as fast as they could reload. The intense soldier's battle raged on, seemingly with a furious, feral momentum of its own. And so, all through the morning, as one historian said, ". . . here on the Confederate right, the struggle was touch and go, until the beginning was unrememberable and no end seemed possible." And so the Confederate flank attack turned into a frontal assault.

Rosecrans had set up his headquarters in a tiny log house on a rise of ground a little west of the LaFayette Road, almost two miles north of Lee and Gordon's Mills. He wore a blue army coat, with a spiffy white vest underneath, black trousers, and his black campaign hat. He moved about the headquarters area with an easy confidence, smiling and chipper; after days of perilous uncertainty, the battle had begun, and his troops were doing all that he intended: they were holding. At one point, he paused to chat with a Rebel prisoner, a Texas captain from Hood's outfit, the latter's presence revealing that some of Longstreet's corps from Virginia had already reached the battlefield. Rosecrans estimated that Longstreet was bringing 17,000 fresh, jaunty Eastern troops to reinforce Bragg's army; but, at least outwardly, he seemed singularly unvexed by the prospect. He questioned the captured Texan briefly, but as usual, it was mostly a waste of time. Finally, Rosecrans observed, "Captain, you don't seem to know much, for a man whose appearance seems to indicate so much intelligence." The Texan smiled, and drawled, "Well, General, if you are not satisfied with my information, I will volunteer some. We are going to whip you most tremendously in this fight."

As was his practice, Braxton Bragg remained aloof from the battle once underway. He moved to various points during the morning but did not intervene in the conduct of the battle except to send Ben Cheatham's men to help Walker on the Confederate right against Thomas' men. Bragg was uncertain what to do next. His inclination was, as always, to seek the psychological security of adhering to the original plan, which meant reinforcing the right in order to try

Ohio Volunteers. Numerous regiments from the Buckeye State fought bravely at Chickamauga in what was a confused battle in which units got lost in the woods, orders failed to reach officers, and neither side really knew who was actually winning.

once more to outflank the Union left; but events on that hotly disputed front were not marching to a marvel, and Bragg was considering instead a blow further south, against the Yankee center.

As often happens, events forced the Confederate commander to a decision. Thomas' men seemed to be winning the long, bitter firefight on Bragg's right; Cheatham's men were being slowly pushed back, and the Confederate right flank was once again in danger. Bragg decided to pull one of Buckner's divisions, that of Maj. Gen. Alexander P. Stewart, from the left of his line, and send it north to support the right flank. A hard-hitting West Pointer from Tennessee, Stewart was called "Old Straight" by his troops, a nickname he had acquired at the Military Academy when he taught mathematics there, and one that seemed appropriate because of his rigidly upright posture.

Stewart, a bright officer, was troubled by the vagueness of Bragg's orders to reinforce the right. He wanted to know, where, exactly, was he to take his men into the fight. Bragg, who did not—could not—know exactly what the situation was in those dark, chaotic woods to the north, was unable to enlighten Stewart. Bragg told him to check with Bishop Polk, who might know more precisely. But Polk was nowhere about. In disgust, Stewart led his division around past the rear of Hood's units, marching downstream through the dusky, quiet, woods. At about 1430 hours, he turned his command west, and moved his men forward to attack. But Stewart and his men were a full mile south of

where Bragg wished to deploy him against Thomas' corps; Stewart's attack struck Crittenden's men instead.

Horatio P. VanCleve commanded the Third Division of Crittenden's III Corps. An unexpected attack on his troops by Alexander P. Stuart's Confederates almost catapulted the Union Army into disaster on the first day.

The bluejacketed infantrymen of Brig. Gen. Horatio P. Van Cleve's *3rd Division* of *XXI Corps* were at last at rest, after two nights of wearying marches. They were tired, and thankful that, as the sound of guns to the north told them, Thomas' men were being hit by the Rebels instead of themselves. It had been quiet on their front all day, and they did not wish, or expect, that this would change. They were most unready for the shock of a Confederate assault.

John Bell Hood commanded the First Division of Longstreet's corps. He was a master-mind at delivering terrific knockout blows in combat. Hood lost his left arm at Gettysburg and was further crippled by the loss of his right leg at Chickamauga. In 1864, his ill-fated invasion of Tennessee was annihilated by George H. Thomas at Nashville.

Suddenly, Stewart's grayclad infantrymen came whooping and screaming out of the woods upon Van Cleve's unready men. Van Cleve was another of the Civil War's West Point retreads, at 54 the oldest man of his rank in the Union Army; he gamely did what he could to hold his three rattled infantry brigades in line, but he had no chance. His division was overwhelmed in one wild, frantic rush by Stewart's men. There was now a huge hole in the center of the Union line.

Stewart's men rolled across the LaFayette Road to within easy sight of Rosecrans' log cabin headquarters, its yard full of blueclad staff officers and messengers and their mounts. George Thomas, realizing the danger on the south, sent John Brannan's shaky outfit down to tear at the Rebel flank. What happened next was pure good luck.

It will be remembered that two of Thomas' divisions were on the road, marching northwards to join their brethren on the Union left; Reynold's division was out in front, and Negley's was about a mile behind. These providentially were already at hand as Stewart's troops broke through Van Cleve's line. Both divisions were ordered to face right and counterattack against Stewart's men.

Reynolds' and Negley's troops battered back Stewart's men frontally, while fire from Brannan's men tore at the northern edges of the Confederate brigades. Stewart's tough men retreated grudgingly, firing as they moved rearward. The Rebels fell back to cover in the woods about half a mile east of the LaFayette Road. They then put out a vigorous, slashing fire against the Yankees coming at them from out in the open; the bluecoated infantrymen paused uncertainly, and then fell back, content to have reestablished the Union defense line.

All of this time, doughty, one-armed John Bell Hood waited just a little south of Stewart, without orders. Had Hood's two divisions and Buckner's one been ordered to support Stewart's assault with an attack of their own at the outset, they might well have overrun Crittenden's line and caught Reynolds' and Negley's divisions vulnerable in line of march. The Rebels could have won the Battle of Chickamauga on the first day, in the center, not on the right. But Bragg's rigidity and indecisiveness precluded such a rapid shift of emphasis and made it hard to mount coordinated, instead of piecemeal, assaults. Perhaps even more crucial was the claustrophobic nature of the woodland terrain in which the fierce battle raged. The commanders did not—could not—know where their units were; after all, Stewart's breakthrough was one of those fortuitous accidents so frequent in the chaos of infantry combat; he had struck at the right place by mistake, and neither Bragg nor Polk had the remotest concept of where he was at his moment of greatest success. Yet it is also fair to say that, with all of the Yankee reinforcements flowing northward to support Thomas, Bragg should have realized that Rosecrans' army must be very vulnerable in its middle.

At about 1600, though still without orders, Hood deployed his two divisions in line, Bushrod Johnson's on the left and Brig. Gen. Evander M. Law's on the right, and started them through the woods westward toward the Yankees, stimulated by the heavy firing at the height of Stewart's action. On the far right, a Texas brigade

Bushrod R. Johnson.

passed through the remnants of a battered Tennessee regiment. The worn-out Tennesseans were sitting and lying in the brush, sweating and panting from fear and exertion. One of the Texans, with the cockiness of the yet unbloodied, shouted imperiously, "Rise up, Tennesseans, and see the Texans go in!" The winded Vols just stared hard-eyed at the gray backs of the advancing Texas infantry.

Hood's men were hard, tough fighters, used to success in the Army of Northern Virginia. They came scrambling out of the trees and brush not far from the LaFayette Road, about a mile south of where Stewart's men had been an hour past. Shouting and whooping, they headed straight toward a lone Yankee division lined up along the west side of the road.

The bluejacketed infantry were the three brigades of Brig. Gen. Jefferson C. Davis' *1st Division* of McCook's *XX Corps*. They had no help on either flank, and were outnumbered two-to-one by the hard-charging Rebels. The Yankee infantry fired hastily, feeling the pressure of the onrushing Gray swarm, spreading out in front and to both sides of them; shakily, they poured out a heavy, but inaccurate, fire. Both menaced flanks collapsed at once, then the center gave way, too. Another huge hole had opened in the middle of Rosecrans' front, and for the second time this day, Confederate infantrymen chased a disintegrating Yankee division to within sight of Old Rosy's command post. And so once again, the Confederates had a chance to win the Battle of Chickamauga on the first day in the center of the Union line.

There were two more Rebel divisions in the vicinity of Hood's troops: one of Buckner's divi-

Evander M. Law

sions, to the south; and Hindman's division, sent across the Chickamauga an hour before to be held as a reserve, in the rear. Both units heard the crackling, electric din of sustained rifle fire from the front, but without orders, neither Buckner nor Hindman was willing to take the risk of moving forward in support of Hood. Basically, no single individual was in tactical command of the forces in the center of the Confederate front.

Menawhile, Bragg was still very much troubled over the unsatisfactory state of affairs on his right flank. At about 1500, he had finally decided that Hill's command should be more than spectators in the battle; so he detached fighting Pat Cleburne's division from Hill's corps and ordered it to the right to support Polk, who—somewhere to the rear of Walker—was ostensibly in command on that flank. Cleburne's men waded the icy, chesthigh creek, and reached the west bank not far from Hood's units, who, judging by the din to westward, were now clearly engaged in a huge scrap. Cleburne obeyed his orders and proceeded north to locate Bishop Polk.

Thus it was that Hood's two aggressive divisions surged, victorious, but unsupported, across the LaFayette Road. And once again, Old Rosy proved a lucky man, for just then there appeared from the south long lines of marching men in blue, heading north from Lee and Gordon's Mill. They were Brig. Gen. Thomas J. Wood's *1st Division*, of Crittenden's *XXI Corps*, moving up to join their fellow units in the center of Rosecrans' front. Wood's brigades streamed against Hood's open left flank, where there was no support from Buckner. Johnson halted his

Jefferson C. Davis

John B. Hood (1831–1893)

A native of Kentucky, Hood graduated from West Point 44th in the class of 1853, and entered the infantry. He served in garrison and on the frontier, where he was wounded, before resigning from the army as a first lieutenant in April of 1861. He immediately entered Confederate service in the same rank. He held a variety of minor commands with some distinction until the Peninsular Campaign, when he was named brigadier general and given a brigade of Texans which he led with skill and verve at Gaines' Mills and thereafter in the Second Bull Run and Antietam Campaigns. In October of 1862 he was named major general and given a division in Longstreet's I Corps. He led his division at Fredericksburg, in the Carolinas, and at Gettysburg, his division making the principal Confederate attack on 2 July which almost destroyed the *Army of the Potomac*, during which his left arm was crippled. He went west with Longstreet's corps later in 1863,

briefly commanding it and several divisions of the Army of Tennessee at Chickamauga, where he lost his right leg. Remaining in the West, he was given a corps in the Army of Tennessee by Joe Johnston and promoted to lieutenant general. He led his corps with commendable aggressiveness in the opening stages of the Atlanta Campaign, during which Johnston's clever maneuvering kept Federal gains to a minimum, but proved bad for Confederate morale. In July Hood was

made an acting general, superceding Johnston in command, an action dictated by Jefferson Davis' dissatisfaction over Johnston's refusal to fight. Hood did fight, but Sherman won all the battles, securing Atlanta and ultimately launching his famed "March to the Sea." In a desperate move, Hood launched his army into Tennessee, hoping to divert Sherman's attention, but was himself defeated by Thomas at Nashville. Relieved at his own request, he reverted to his permanent rank but saw no further service. After the war he became a merchant in New Orleans, married and had eleven children in ten years, and wrote his memoirs. The yellow fever epidemic of 1878 caused a financial crisis which wiped out his fortune and, in the following year carried off him, his wife, and one of their children. A big, aggressive man who loved combat, Hood was not a subtle commander and had an unfortunate tendency to blame his subordinates for his own errors.

units' forward momentum in order to redeploy them to face both west and south. With Johnson stopped, Law, on the right, also halted his division's advance, in order not to expose his units' flanks. Meanwhile, Davis had reestablished control over his straggled troops, and led them back to strike Hood's units as best they could after their earlier rough handling. Hood's assault was stopped, but for how long none could say; knocked temporarily back on their heels by the sudden, surprising Union recovery, Hood's jaunty, aggressive soldiers expected to shortly dominate their opponents and drive them again to the rear. Both forces sought to build up fire superiority, the Yankees in order to better hold, the Rebels in order to successfully charge.

At this most opportune moment, pugnacious Phil Sheridan's tough *3rd Division*, of McCook's *XX Corps*, following behind Wood's outfit on the road north, arrived at the scene of battle. Little

Phil quickly flung his brigades into the melee, and their extra numbers and firepower gained the Union forces the advantage needed to drive Hood's two divisions backwards, though not too far. The Confederates were displaced only to the right side of the road. When Sheridan's aggressive troops tried to drive them further back, the Rebel infantry smashed them with torrents of heavy, well-aimed fire. In all, Hood's divisions had gained about a mile.

On the right of Hood's line, the Texas brigade retreated back to the same woods from which they had advanced such a short time past. Rosecrans had retained John Wilder's formidable brigade of mounted infantry from Maj. Gen. Joseph J. Reynolds' *4th Division, XIV Corps*, as a mobile reserve because of the high firepower of its repeating carbines; and he had sent these aggressive men to contain Hood's advance. There, on the far right of Hood's line, they had shot the Texans bloody. Now, having had all they wanted of the battle, the chastened Texans once again moved past the rested Tennesseans; one of the Vols shouted sardonically, "Rise up, Tennesseans, and see the Texans come out!" And so the unsupported assaults of Hood's game men were stopped.

The battle in the center, like that in the north, continued randomly, fitfully, as the day wore on. A soldier in the 1st Tennessee Infantry had had such a strong premonition of death prior to his unit's assault that he refused to eat, distributed his possessions to his friends, and readied his personal effects to be sent home to his family. Yet he fought on throughout the long day of fierce battle unhurt. Now at rest in the brush, a friend said to him, "Bob, you weren't killed, as you expected." Just then, a solid iron cannon shot slammed into the worried soldier, and slaughtered him. Yet, as always in combat, others with equally intense premonitions of death fought hard all day, and while many friends died around them, survived as if charmed.

One of Hood's hard-bitten young Texans, hit in the foot, dragged himself out of the fight and managed to hop on his good foot back to a field hospital. Laid out on a table, he was told by a blood-stained surgeon that gangrene would kill him if his foot were not amputated soon. The Texan drew back his good leg, and kicked the doctor hard, knocking him backwards; then he fled, hobbling back to the front where he deemed it safer. His buddies looked after him, regularly dousing his wound with acid, and he lived to recover fully.

A Georgia infantryman was hit by a Yankee round full in the chest; the impact knocked him unconscious, and his buddies assumed that he was dead. Later, it was discovered that he was still breathing, and he was brought to the doctors. The man was a medical anomoly, a rare case in which the heart and abdominal organs were transposed at birth. The Confederate army doctors did not realize this. Amazed to find the man alive at all, and his heart beating normally, after having been shot directly in the chest, they were even more astounded to note that his heart was on the right side of his body. They erroneously concluded that his heart had been knocked from the left to the right side of his torso by the impact of the minie ball that had struck him. So he became famous in the army and afterwards throughout a long, healthy life as "the man whose heart was knocked to the wrong side at Chickamauga."

Philip Henry Sheridan commanded the Third Division of McCook's XX Corps. Sheridan's main claim to fame was his destructive march down the Shenandoah Valley, where he decisively defeated a Confederate force led by Jubal Early at Cedar Creek. On the second day of Chickamauga, his force was caught up in the rout caused by the Rebel breakthrough in the Union line.

Meanwhile, Pat Cleburne's chilled, wet men reached Polk's command post, behind Walker's front on the right of the Confederate line. They moved up to replace Walker's tired troops in the assault. Walker's worn men cheered, both in admiration and in thanks that they would not have to go in again themselves, as Cleburne's ever precisely-ordered ranks of infantry moved past in the dusk, ready for one last try that day at Thomas' front.

Thomas now held the northern end of the Union line with five divisions, as Reynolds' outfit had come up. Negley's division, however, had been forced to remain back in the center of the Union line to help seal the hole that Stewart's and Hood's divisions had ripped open between the units of Crittenden and McCook.

Sage, seasoned, strapping, Ol' Pap Thomas smelled another Rebel attack. His troops thought—and hoped—that he was wrong; it

was getting too dark, and even the tenacious Rebels must have had enough of battle by now. But Thomas was insistent. He had the divisions of Baird and Richard Johnson—of McCook's corps—in line furthest north, and he warned them both to be ready. The divisions of Palmer—of Crittenden's corps—and Reynolds and Brannan (in that order, from north to south) held the remainder of Thomas' front. Slowly the sun went down, orange-red, beyond the dark hump of Missionary Ridge; Thomas' men thought that, for once, their steady boss had been wrong.

Then in the fading twilight, Pat Cleburne's tough, able young men, three brigades strong, came roaring out of the dark woods in line abreast. And Ben Cheatham's hard-fighting units came on right behind them. It was a compact, powerful blow. Cleburne's men were screaming shrilly and firing rapidly, winking

Federals repulse a Confederate attack.

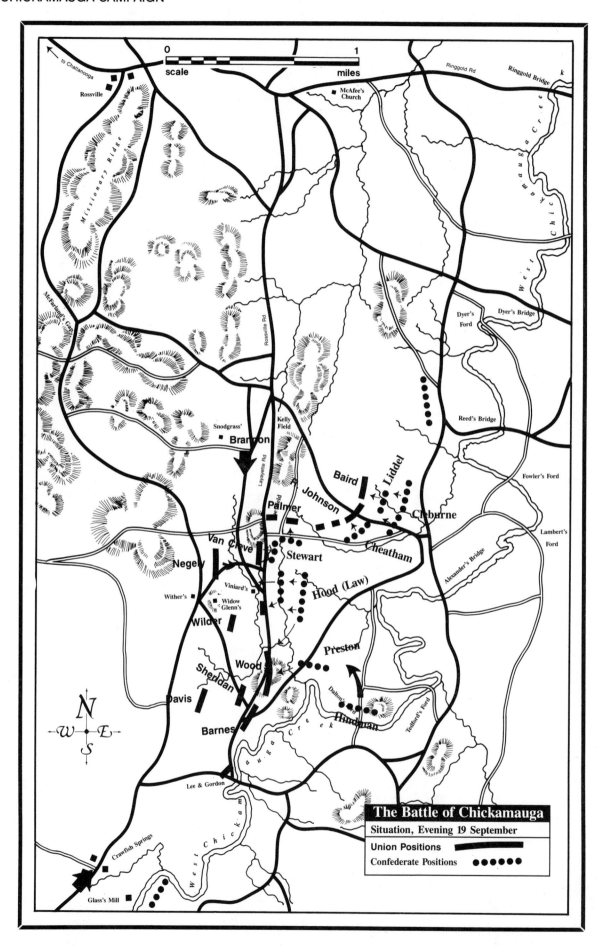

The Battle of Chickamauga
Situation, Evening 19 September
Union Positions
Confederate Positions

red flashes in the deepening purplish dusk, as they charged wildly forward. Always well-trained by their capable commander, they knew how to maneuver best to mass their heavy, well-aimed fire. Cleburne thought that their fire this night was the heaviest he had ever seen. At the receiving end of those flashing rifles, an Indiana infantry captain agreed, writing later that Cleburne's troops were "loading and firing in a manner that I believe was never surpassed on any battlefield during the rebellion."

Baird's units and Brannan's hard-used men were flung back almost a mile by this last, mad Confederate charge; but the units in the center of Thomas' line gave less ground, so that they projected outward in a salient several hundred yards in advance of the two flank divisions. The Confederate charge was stopped well short of the LaFayette Road by greater numbers, dense forest, and the onset of darkness. Cleburne's men were brave and game, and they fought hard and well indeed, but, like Hood's men before, they simply were not strong enough to succeed in the kind of piecemeal, unsupported assaults into which their reckless and unwise chief, at once rigid and indecisive, and his unimaginative subordinates, insisted on plunging them. Such good men deserved better from their leaders.

So ended the first long, fierce day of the Battle of Chickamauga. And the night fell, grim and frosty.

Night, 19–20 September

The battle died hard—random shots rang out in the silent, frosty, smoky forest until 2300 hours.

Bragg deemed the day's fierce, furious combat of his army as merely "severe skirmishing . . . while endeavoring to get into line of battle." Cranky Harvey Hill, his worst forebodings of this curious Western army now realized, disgustedly evaluated his chief's clumsy, piecemeal tactics as "the sparring of the amateur boxer, not the crushing blows of the trained pugilist."

That night, Bragg decided to reorganize his army, an unusual occurrence in the face of the enemy, and one for which he has been much criticized by historians. Yet the great Confederate failing on that first day had been an utter lack of centralized direction; at crucial points in the battle, each corps commander had done as his judgment dictated, with the result that some chose to attack and others chose to await explicit orders, producing a disastrous series of uncoordinated, unsupported assaults. Surely, Bragg, who could not be everywhere on the battlefield, and whose indecisiveness in any case did not dispose him to intervene forcibly and directly in a battle once commenced, was not wrong to try to impose greater control and coordination upon his corps commanders, at least to the degree permitted by the tangled terrain. He decided to divide the army into two wings: the right wing of five divisions to be commanded by Polk, and the left wing of six divisions to be commanded by the imminently expected Longstreet. This design necessitated some confused shifting of corps and division alignments during the night; and it meant entrusting half the battle to the command of a man who had never seen the battlefield by daylight, but it was a major improvement in command arrangements.

Tactically, Bragg's rigidity, his inveterate desire to seek inner peace in the security of a fixed design to which he could revert in time of stress and turmoil, made him determined—despite the fact that his army had twice during the day nearly broken through the weakened enemy center while gaining little ground against his strong left—to try to carry out his original plan of outflanking and driving in the Union left; as he put it, "to turn the enemy's left, and by direct attack force him into McLemore's Cove," pinned against the mountains on all sides. To this end, he deployed Breckinridge's division on his far right flank, north of Cleburne's division, in front of Reed's Bridge, trying futilely to extend his line to overlap Thomas' northern flank. Yet in this design, Bragg was endeavoring to attack the strongest portion of Rosecrans' front with the weakest half of his own army.

Bragg had better choices, two of them in fact. He might have made his main assault against the more vulnerable enemy center. Or, had he possessed more daring, and trusted his commanders better, he might have tried to shift his army northward, not merely to hammer at

Thomas' left flank, but to strike for the mountain passes a few scant miles westward and cut Rosecrans' army off from its base at Chattanooga. Instead, he did as he invariably did when forced to think hard under great pressure; he reverted to his original plan. The Army of Tennessee would strike hard on the right at daylight in successive attacks spreading from north to south all along the line until Longstreet's left wing divisions joined in successively, pinning the Union reserves, and placing great pressure on the Union front, enabling Polk's right wing to envelop the Union left and Longstreet's wing to smash through the Union center. Polk's wing would then move southward, as would also Longstreet's wing, to drive the Yankees against the Desolate Mountains to the south.

So Bragg planned. But his plans would almost immediately began to be undermined by an old vice, the utter lack of command and control in his Army of Tennessee.

Bragg told Polk that he was to have Hill's corps, Walker's corps, and Cheatham's division attack in succession on the right wing at daylight. He issued no written orders. He left entirely to Polk's dubious initiative the task of passing the orders on to the subordinate generals, and he did not have his staff check to make sure that the corps and division commanders had indeed received their orders.

When Bragg went to sleep in his ambulance at his headquarter's camp near Alexander's Bridge, Longstreet had not yet arrived from Catoosa Station, and his two corps commanders on the left wing, Hood and Buckner, had received no orders for the morrow at all. And so the skein of Bragg's unimaginative plan very quickly commenced to unravel.

Longstreet's train arrived in the afternoon unmet by any representative of Bragg. "Ol' Pete" and his staff had to wait for their horses to be brought up on a later train while they listened to the distant thunder of the battle to westward.

Yankee wounded arrive at the Army of the Cumberland's supply depot in Stevenson, Alabama. Over 34,000 Union and Confederate soldiers were killed or wounded at Chickamauga making it one of the bloodiest battles of the war.

The burly, independent Georgian was already disgruntled. Bragg had yet another prima donna—but this time a capable one—coming to join his command.

Longstreet and two of his officers, mounted at last, grimly picked their way over narrow roads through the darkening forest, trying to find their way to Bragg by heeding the unreliable directions of civilians, listening for the sound of guns, and at last, following the track of wounded men drifting rearward. Suddenly, ahead of them in the dark, came a brisk shout of challenge. They identified themselves as friends. But in the course of the shouted conversation in the dark, the picket soldier gave the number of his unit. Longstreet started—Confederate soldiers identified their units by the names of their commanders, only Union troops customarily identified their units by numbers. Longstreet and his staff had blundered into a Yankee outpost. Tentatively, trying to disguise his Georgia drawl and also sound casual, Ol' Peter said, "Let us ride down a little way to find a better crossing." Then the three grayclad horsemen rode slowly away, afraid to breath deeply, waiting for the sound of bullets at their back; yet none were fired.

The three wandering Rebels finally located Bragg and roused him for a brief conference in which he explained the outline of his plan and Longstreet's large role in its execution. Tired and glum, Longstreet made no attempt to locate Hood and Buckner in the dark; so his two corps commanders still had received no orders for the next day. Longstreet went to sleep on branches cut from trees.

Meanwhile, sulking Harvey Hill had wandered briefly through the dark, smoky woods, also in search of Bragg. When he failed to find him quickly, he gave up the quest; he was tired and decided to rest a while before seeking out Polk. A dense, clamy fog drifted in, further curtailing visibility in the smoke and dark. Hill did not strain himself looking for Polk. It seems evident that the prickly, disgruntled Hill was acting irresponsibly; sulking, he wanted no part of more orders from Braxton Bragg. Polk sent a messenger with orders for Hill. But by this time the good Bishop, never a genius, was so addled by long service under Braxton Bragg that he could not even perform this simple task well. He did not send a staff officer with the message, but instead sent it via an enlisted man of his own cavalry escort. The man not only could not locate Hill, but he did not inform anyone of this rather important fact. And then the Bishop

Terrain of the Chickamauga battlefield around the Roseville Gap. By the end of the second day of battle, Thomas' troops withdrew through the gap after displaying a gallant defense against larger Confederate forces.

Union supply depot at Stevenson, Alabama. The complete action of Chickamauga took place over a wide area. The goal of the campaign, Chattanooga, was in eastern Tennessee: Chickamauga was fought in northern Georgia, and the Federal supply base was in northern Alabama.

blundered again. It was vital that Breckinridge's division be in proper position promptly, because it was slated to initiate the divisional assaults in succession; the division to the south of it would not attack until after Breckinridge did, and so on down through the entire Confederate line. Until Breckinridge's division attacked, there could be no Confederate attack. Yet after his division crossed the Chickamauga at Alexander's Bridge, Breckinridge asserted that his men were tired—yet they had had no part in the day's battle and it is difficult to understand what had made them so—and requested permission to halt where he was, still one and a half miles from his assigned position in the battle line. Hill had sent a staff officer to guide Breckinridge's outfit, and the young officer sensibly wanted Breckinridge and his men to proceed. But along came Polk. When

possible always courtly to his officers and indulgent to his men, Polk contradicted the staff officer, and allowed Breckinridge to halt his division for the night. Indeed, Polk never mentioned to Breckinridge that he was to commence the army's assault at daylight.

So Bragg's careful establishment of wing commanders did not help in the least; none of his corps commanders knew that they were supposed to attack in the morning. The situation in the Union forces was little better.

Interestingly, despite the fact that the enemy had twice during the day almost crashed through the center of his line not far from where he stood, Rosecrans still fretted about his left; old illusions die hard. So far, Thomas had held; and Halleck was promising reinforcements. But he still did not know what to do except to hold.

self with little, impromptu catnaps. So now the large, placid Virginian slept lightly, floating restfully but not obliviously through the conference, as he had done during a similar crisis at Murfreesboro; fitfully he awoke, always to express the same opinion, "I would strengthen the left." Rosecrans asked, "Where are we going to take it from?" and the question hung in the close air unanswered and unanswerable.

The decision, as at Murfreesboro, was that the *Army of the Cumberland* had to hold. No one wished to undertake the grave risk of a night retreat, with the grim possibility that the army might be caught as it fled westward, strung out in marching columns slowed by the wagons of its vast supply train, and readily destroyed; and no one wished to attack the hard-fighting and more numerous Rebels. The army would—had to—hold.

Rosecrans decided to shorten his line and concentrate his forces even more. Thomas was to continue to hold with his five divisions on the left, with Negley's division, never having quite made it all the way north, deployed to his right (south); McCook was to move his two divisions northward to link up with Negley's outfit, while Crittenden's two divisions were pulled from the line to be held in close reserve to support the Union center or be shifted to the left as need decreed. Rosecrans did not bring up Granger's small *Reserve Corps;* he wanted to keep that at Rossville to hold open the gap in the mountains and the road back toward Chattanooga in case of defeat.

The commanding general then graciously served coffee, while McCook entertained the officers with a plaintive rendition of a long, sentimental ballad.

George Thomas did not get back to his command until 0200 hours, but his task was still not done. He had kept his tired men hard at work constructing defensive breastworks in front of their positions. Surprisingly, the men did not complain at these new exertions. They had seen the wild fury of the last assault by Cleburne's men, and they feared what they would face in the morning. Besides, most of them lacked blankets, and it was cold in the dank, foggy forest that long night, so the exercise warmed them, and the physical exertion was therapy for minds troubled by fearsome thoughts. Thomas found at his command post a note from Baird. Baird warned that if he tried, as ordered, to keep his left extended as far north as the road from Reed's Bridge, his division would be stretched too thin to have much chance of beating off

He decided to call a command conference in order to hear the opinions of—and share the responsibility with—his corps commanders.

The conference began in the log cabin at about 2300. The corps commanders had little to contribute. The congenial, ruddy McCook and hearty Crittenden, with his dreamy eyes and trim mustache—both likeable but unlucky officers—were not about to offer much advice to their moody, exacting chief; they had each lost a division to Thomas, and been hit hard in the center. It was unfortunate that they were not more voluble this night; perhaps a recital of their troubles might have shifted Rosecrans' focus from the north to the center of his line.

Thomas was very tired after two nights of rapid movement and a day of heavy battle. But he had the old soldier's facility of restoring him-

another of the Confederate's hard, fierce frontal assaults. Despite his weariness, Thomas, a most wise and experienced officer, did not seek to dampen his subordinate's fears with lulling platitudes so that he could get to sleep. Instead, he went out into the forest to see for himself. And what he saw was that Baird was emphatically correct.

Thomas immediately contacted Rosecrans, requesting that Negley's division be sent to rejoin his corps so tht he could extend his critical left flank. Rosecrans, as ever concerned about his left, readily agreed; for he knew Thomas to be a man of careful, but shrewd, judgment. Negley was ordered to march north at dawn. And George Henry Thomas at last lay down to sleep under a large oak tree whose protruding roots served as his pillow.

The stage was now set for the second day of Chickamauga.

Alert Yankees guard against approaching camouflaged Confederate skirmishers.

The Second Day, 2d September 1863

Slowly, the deep, shiny red disc of the sun rose above the hazy woods, heralding a new day, 20 September 1863, a Sunday. One Union officer thought its color symbolic. Pointing to the sun, he said, "This will indeed be a day of blood."

Thomas glanced often at the lightening sky, wondering when Negley would arrive to help protect his vulnerable left flank.

Rosecrans rode along Thomas' line, as he had at Murfreesboro, to cheer and inspire his troops. He spoke confidently, but his strong face looked pinched and puffy from too little sleep and too much concealed worry. He told his soldiers, "Fight today as well as you did yesterday, and we shall whip them!"

The dense morning fog, mixed with the lingering bluer gray haze of the previous day's gunsmoke and deeper gray coils of smoke from numerous fires ignited in the dry forest by yesterday's gunblasts, suffused the woods in a chill, eerie gray glow. More and more men stirred, then woke; they ate and then waited quietly in both dread and hope in the hush of the dense haze.

Braxton Bragg, better rested than night owl Rosecrans, was up early, too—before dawn. After so much frustration, he could not wait to hear the sudden thunder of the Confederate guns firing in support of Polk's assault; little did he realize that his corps commanders had not yet been informed that they were to attack. So Bragg waited. And nothing happened. Increasingly anxious and bitterly disappointed, Bragg sent a staff officer to find Polk to "ascertain the cause of the delay and urge him to a prompt and speedy movement."

Polk, meanwhile, had at last learned from his defective courier that he had been unable to locate Hill during the night. The Bishop, at last spurred to a semblance of concern, decided to bypass the peripatetic corps commander and issued orders directly to Hill's division commanders, John Breckinridge and Pat Cleburne. He told them by messenger to "move and attack the enemy as soon as you are in position." The good Bishop then paused for breakfast before heading for the front.

Harvey Hill was with Breckinridge and Cleburne when they received Polk's message. Brekinridge's wagons had gotten lost during the night movement, and some of his men had not eaten since before the previous day's battle. Hill was also very much concerned with the breastworks that Thomas' enterprising men had constructed in front of their defensive positions during the night; he did not think that his two divisions, attacking singly side-by-side would be strong enough to break through such defenses, and he wanted time to think of an alternative.

Thus, when Breckinridge insisted that his men must be fed breakfast before attacking, Hill agreed with him. After all, Polk's message did not specify an attack at daybreak, but merely when Hill's divisions were ready. Hill wrote out a note for Polk informing him that it would be "an hour or more" before his divisions would be able to attack; he also said that he did not think it was possible for his men to take the enemy position; it was too strong, and they were too few.

While Bishop Polk awaited breakfast, he perused a newspaper; and so Bragg's staff emissary found him. Learning of this, Bragg screamed out a rare profanity, and headed for Polk's headquarters, which, as usual, was functioning more like a hindquarters. However, before Bragg arrived, Polk was jolted from his complacency by the note from Hill. Hill's pessimism depressed Polk, and he decided to go forward to see for himself the situation at the front. He considerately left a verbal message for Bragg as he departed, saying to an aide, "Do tell General Bragg that my heart is overflowing with anxiety for the attack. Overflowing with anxiety, sir."

Bragg found Hill before Polk did. He confronted the touchy corps commander and asked him curtly why he had not attacked at daybreak in accordance with his orders. Hill, calm as a lawyer who knows his case is strong, replied smugly that he "was hearing then for the first time that such an order had been issued," and added the additional little dig that he "had not known whether we were to be the assailants or the assailed." Exasperated, Bragg angrily ordered Hill to attack as soon as possible. But while Bragg impatiently fumed, Hill deliberately took plenty of time in organizing his attack, enjoying the torment of his commanding officer. And he made sure that Brekinridge and Cleburne took plenty of time, too. The troops were meticulously aligned in their jump-off positions in the woods; ammunition pouches were carefully checked. The three officers did

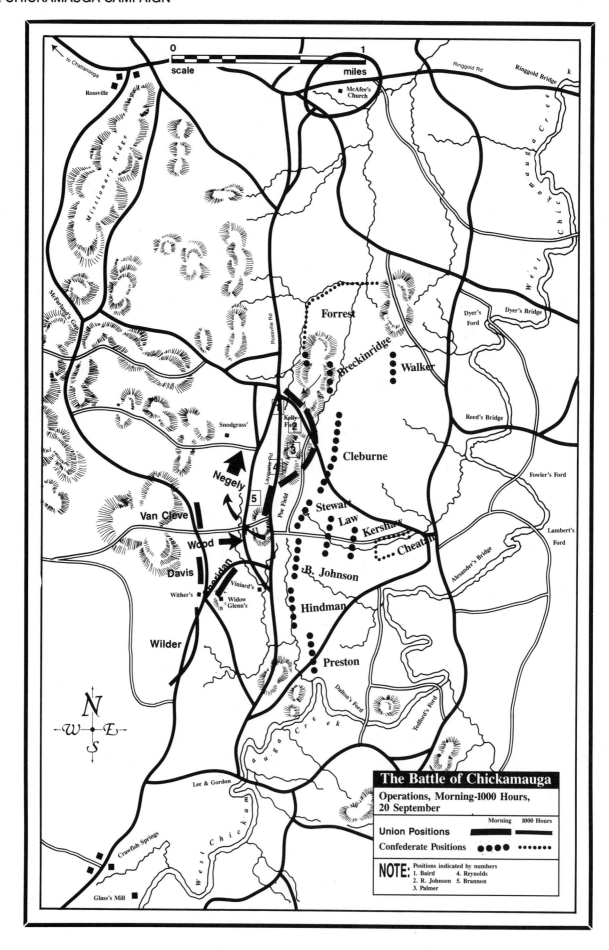

The Battle of Chickamauga

Operations, Morning-1000 Hours, 20 September

	Morning	1000 Hours
Union Positions	▬▬▬	▬▬▬
Confederate Positions	●●●●	•••••••

NOTE: Positions indicated by numbers
1. Baird   4. Reynolds
2. R. Johnson   5. Brannon
3. Palmer

everything by the book, a spiteful joke on the punctilious Bragg.

It was 0930—over three hours late—when Harvey Hill calmly nodded his head at John Breckinridge, and the Kentuckian's troops stepped out through the trees, tensely headed toward Thomas' log breastworks.

Old Rosy's morning had been less troubled than Bragg's, although, it too, was not without its frustrations.

Rosecrans found the usually placid, reserved Thomas in uncharacteristic gleeful high spirits. Thomas spoke exuberantly, almost boastfully, of the previous day's fighting, telling his boss, "Whenever I touched their flanks they broke, General. They broke!" Thomas' mood was no doubt caused by the failure of the Confederates to resume their assault on his front. As the morning minutes passed in quiet, he had begun to think that the Rebels might have had enough the day before and wanted no more today.

Then as if fearful of tempting fate further by premature chortling, Thomas reverted to his wiser, cautious persona. He warned Rosecrans that his patrols were reporting that the Rebels to their front were continuing to sidle northward, trying to overlap his left flank. Rosecrans, still sensitive about his left, quickly said, "You must move up, too, as fast as they do." Thomas concurred; then he made his point. This required additional troops, and that was the problem; Tom Negley's dilatory division had not yet arrived to reinforce his line. Rosecrans reassured Thomas as to the coming of Negley and his men; Rosecrans had personally got Negley's outfit on the move as he rode up the line to cheer the men and chat with Thomas. Thomas seemed soothed to hear this good news, but remarked cautiously that he could not deem his left flank secure until he had more men to extend it and bulk it up some. Rosecrans departed soon afterward.

Old Rosy was riding past the center of his line when he saw something that set off one of his famous rapid rages. Negley's command—which he had ordered north an hour ago and had just assured Thomas was well on its way to him—was still firmly in place in its old positions. Rosecrans confronted Tom Negley, who had an intelligent explanation of his procrastination. With Crittenden's two divisions pulled back out of the center of the Union line, McCook's corps was supposed to sidle north to fill the gap. McCook's men had not arrived. If Negley had blindly followed his chief's orders to march north, it would have resulted in a mile-long gap in the center of the Federal line.

Irately, Rosecrans rode to the rear, found Crittenden, and instructed him to send Tom Wood's division back into the center of the line to replace Negley's units, who would then march north two miles to help out Thomas. Then Old Rosy dashed southward to seek the tardy McCook and hurry him up. He quickly did so, and then returned northward.

But when he came back opposite the center of his line, he saw that Negley's three brigades were still in the same place he had already left them twice earlier on this day with orders to move on; Wood's men had not yet moved up to replace them in line! Rosecrans told Negley to immediately send one of his brigades up to Thomas. Then he rode madly to the rear to find Wood, rage burning fiercely at the base of his throat.

Wood, a doughty West Point Kentuckian, was conferring with his staff about the division's unexpected orders to move, when the frustrated, furious Rosecrans galloped up to the knot of officers. Forgetting all soldierly protocol in his distemper, Old Rosy roared, "What is the meaning of this, sir?" And before Wood could respond, Rosecrans added bitterly, "You have disobeyed my specific orders. By your damnable negligence you are endangering the safety of the entire army, and by God I will not tolerate it!" Wood reddened at receiving such abuse in front of his officers, who shifted their feet uncomfortably, averting their eyes, endeavoring to pretend that nothing unusual was taking place in their midst. Then Rosecrans said tightly, "Move your division at once, as I have instructed, or the consequences will not be pleasant for yourself." Wood, containing his hurt feelings, saluted.

At about 0945 hours Tom Wood's lead brigade moved into line in Negley's position, as Negley was preparing to rush his two remaining brigades northward. Then, from the north, came the sounds of a huge, crackling, thunderous din. Negley looked up. The Rebels were hitting Old Pap Thomas' men again, and from the sound of it, hitting hard. Tom Negley's thoughts were mixed as he waited to be relieved by Wood and his men. He hoped that Wood's troops moved fast, for Thomas was surely to be in need of help; but he could not have been anxious to take his fine youngsters into that fiery, rumbling hell to the north.

Harvey Hill was right. The Confederate attack did not have the depth to overcome Thomas' strong improvised defenses. But as Rosecrans and Thomas had feared all along, the extreme

The hard-pressed left flank of the Army of the Cumberland holds its position though outnumbered by Confederates under Polk's command. Thomas' XIV Corps refused to give ground throughout the course of the battle. Even after the rest of the Union Army collapsed, the Rock of Chickamauga maintained a spirited defense on Snodgrass Hill which saved the rest of the army from disaster.

left of the Union line was vulnerable; to extend the line northward in the absence of Negley's division, Thomas had sent one of Johnson's brigades from his center to the far left, and then, when Negley's first brigade arrived pursuant to Rosecrans' direct order, Thomas deployed it to the left of Johnson's brigade. But these two brigades had not had time to construct log defenseworks; thus, they had no cover, and Breckinridge's two northernmost brigades were able to assault them on equal terms. The two Gray brigades advanced and opened a heavy fire against Johnson's and Negley's men. The Yankee fire was a little less brisk, and soon the Rebels achieved fire superiority. Then the Union brigades began to buckle a little. Breckenridge's men charged furiously forward. The Yankees fell back. The two Rebel brigades reached the LaFayette Road, and then turned south to strike Thomas' line in flank, illustrating that had Bragg attempted to amass greater strength on the extreme northern flank of his line, he might have been able to win the battle exactly as he had planned; once again, Bragg's tactical clumsiness had vitiated a viable plan of battle. Yet it appeared that Thomas' left flank was now open and exposed.

But Thomas, moving his units with the desperate intensity of a one-armed circus juggler with too many balls in the air, took one of Brannan's shaky brigades from the right of his line and ordered it flung in on the left. At the same time, an unexpected boon turned up; one of Van Cleve's brigades, so harshly used by the Rebels the day before, arrived. Rosecrans, always sure and decisive in his intentions as to his left flank, had ordered this brigade to march double-time to Thomas as soon as he heard the first din of the Rebel attack. Thomas promptly sent these new men in with Brannan's troops. The two new brigades stopped the Rebel assault with their unexpected fire. Soon Johnson's and Negley's men joined the welcome newcomers, and the Blue infantrymen began to develop strong fire superiority over the increasingly outnumbered Confederates, and then successfully drove them back. The most endangered point of Thomas' line had held. It seemed a great harbinger of victory for the Union cause.

A little to the south, Breckinridge's other brigade had no chance. The Rebels attacked into the north end of the mile-long line of log breastworks erected during the night by the industrious Yankees. Lacking the strength to overrun the Union defensive positions, Breckinridge's men stood in the open, firing, trying to achieve

Benjamin H. Helm.

fire superiority against men concealed and protected by thick logs, a futile task. Baird's infantry readily shot up Breckinridge's men, and sent them reeling back. This left-most brigade of Breckinridge's division was commanded by Brig. Gen. Ben Hardin Helm, brother-in-law and friend of the President of the United States, who would mourn much for him. Helm was killed trying to lead his men forward into the stinging swarm of red flashes from the log barrier ahead, and one-third of his men were down when the rest fell back. This disaster to Breckinridge's men relieved the pressure on the Union left, and allowed Thomas to use his four brigades to the north to keep up their own grinding pressure on Breckinridge's two isolated brigades, which, as the morning wore on, were slowly shoved back with ever increasing casualties. By noon, Breckinridge's division was spent and ruined.

Pat Cleburne's division went in to the south of Breckinridge's men, and as always, attacked ferociously and efficiently; but these fine infantry, too, came to grief against Thomas' logs, and the shattering defensive firepower of protected riflemen. As usual, the attack was poorly coordinated, and Cleburne's right-most brigade did not assault until Helm's outfit, to his left, had already been smashed. The two southernmost of Cleburne's brigades were delayed in the assault by inadvertant contact with Stewart's and Cheatham's men, but when they finally moved up, they too were badly mangled by the intense fire of Baird's and Johnson's protected Blue infantrymen.

But Cleburne's dogged infantry, firing grimly from what protection was afforded by thickets and trees, and seeking an opportunity to renew their assault, maintained pressure on the Union lines. Thomas could spare no more men to go north in case of additional dire events in that quarter.

And meanwhile, D. H. Hill was screaming for support from Walker's corps. Ben Cheatham had his hard-fighting five brigades deployed, ready for assault when Bishop Polk gave him the attack order. Cheatham shouted to his gallant grayclad infantry, "Forward, boys, and give them hell!" And as he had at Murfreesboro, the good Bishop approved the sentiment but not the profanity; he called out to the advancing troops, "Do as General Cheatham says, boys!" But Ben Cheatham's tough young men, too, were torn and hurt by the intense, slashing fire from the Union log breastworks. They went forward bent a little, as men hold their bodies when headed into a storm—in this instance, a storm of fire. Men began dropping to the soft, matted brush of the forest floor, and ripped by fire, the lines of Confederate infantry became more ragged. Cheatham's men fell back to seek cover from the deadly fire from the breastworks ahead.

Soon the Rebel divisions of Gist and Liddell went in, assaulting the rest of Johnson's and Palmer's Yankees, too. As always, the dogged Confederate infantry attacked with vigor, but always, too, in series, not together. John Palmer said primly, "The assaults were repeated with an impetuosity that threatened to overwhelm us." An Ohio infantry captain wrote, more to the point, "The rebs charged in three distinct lines, but each time they charged they were driven back with fearfully decimated ranks." These uncoordinated charges into the strength of the Union defenses were doomed. As Harvey Hill understood, the best—indeed, the only—chance for Confederate success on Bragg's right wing this day was on the far north of Breckridge's line, where the Yankee defenses were not strong and some early success had been gleaned. But that was not the plan. Bragg

had ordered a series of sequential attacks all along the line, and Bishop Polk did not think that he could further provoke the ire of his choleric boss by halting his specifically ordered assaults in order to try to re-deploy units to the north; it would disrupt the entire plan of battle, and, by taking pressure off the Yankees for a time, jeopardize the attack of Longstreet's wing. Only Bragg could take upon himself such a momentous decision. But Bragg, as usual, isolated himself from the conduct of a commenced battle. With Bragg aloof from the fight, and Polk devoid of initiative, it is no wonder that the melee on the Confederate right wing did not march to a marvel of success. Polk's attacks on the strongest segment of the Union line—Thomas commanded nearly two-thirds of Rosecrans' units along Chickamauga Creek; his defenses were the strongest, and his men the most mentally ready to fight, of all the Union troops—were fully stalled.

There were several reasons for the failure of the attacks on the Confederate right wing. One was lack of concentration, the failure to strike hardest at one point; the Confederate attacks were too diffuse and, as Harvey Hill readily realized, lacked depth. As one historian put it, "At no one point along the Confederate right had the issue been pressed to its extremity by

Benjamin Franklin Cheatham served under Polk on the Rebel right.

the mass commitment of reserves to achieve a breakthrough. Rather, the pressure had been equally heavy on all points. . . ." Another flaw was Bragg's tactical clumsiness and rigidity. This made it impossible to re-shape the battle once it had commenced in order to reinforce success rather than failure; the Confederates should have amassed more hitting power at the northernmost end of their line on the far right in order to actually accomplish what Bragg's design envisaged, the overlapping of Thomas' left. As an historian tersely observed, "Instead of making a wider encirclement of Thomas' left, they wasted much power in costly assaults against Thomas' log breastworks." The third reason for Polk's failure was the aforementioned great strength—both physical and psychological—of Thomas' portion of the Union line. The last, and perhaps by no means least, of the causes of the defeat of the Confederate right wing was the superb quality of George H. Thomas as a defensive warrior. Always cool and sharp under great pressure, the big Virginian projected to his men an aura of solid invincible confidence. He understood the vital importance of fixed defenses in a war of the rifle, and he was crisp and decisive in his tactical movements, bringing units from relaxed points to pressure points with unerring good timing; he was not hesitant in his judgments, and so his reinforcements were never too late. So within a short time of the onset of the attack, Polk's units had lost nearly a third of their number, but had little of value to show for the bloody toll.

In the south, on the left wing of Bragg's army, the affairs of the Confederates were managed in a much more professional matter. Sullen Old Peter Longstreet, a most difficult subordinate, was also the most capable of the Confederate commanders on the field this day. Freed to an independence which he so deeply relished—and had never found in the Army of Northern Virginia—by Bragg's lethargic system of command, Longstreet had ample scope to display his hard-hitting tactical skill. And he was helped by having the stronger portion of the Confederate army operating against the weaker portion of the Union army, and as it turned out, also by the good fortune which so often abets the skilled and the bold in war.

The northernmost of Longstreet's divisions of the left wing was Maj. Gen. Alexander Stewart's, whose hard-charging men had broken through the Union line the day before. But this time Old Straight's boys headed right into a buzz-saw of fire that cut and chewed them

Alexander P. Stewart.

bloody. For here was the end of Thomas' line, Reynolds' division and Brannan's remaining brigades, the former jutting about 100 yards forward, for Brannan had wisely pulled his outfit a little back to take advantage of the concealment of a copse of thick woods fronting a cleared field, which formed a natural killing ground. Stewart's men came on tenaciously, but could make no headway against the intense fire of Reynolds' and Brannan's men who were well sited and protected by breastworks. Stewart's mangled outfits, like Bishop Polk's before them a little to the north had to fall back and try to sustain a long-range firefight against better protected men, a losing proposition that was producing a steady seepage of blood that threatened to soon render Bragg's army anemic.

While it seemed that the best that Old Straight's men could do was to force the Yankees to keep their heads below the logs when they reloaded and hasten their shots when they reappeared to fire, Stewart's readily beaten offensive nevertheless added to the Union commanders' conviction that Bragg intended to use his entire army against Thomas' flank. It certainly seemed so to Thomas and his men, as they bore the full brunt of the battle and wondered with the justifiable paranoia of all hard-tested combat infantry just what—if anything—the rest of the army was doing to earn its bacon, beans, and hardtack. So Thomas, in his one errant judgment of the day, cried before he was badly hurt, and kept dunning Rosecrans for more troops.

Rosecrans was still very willing to sustain Thomas at virtually any price; for, like Bragg, he estimated that a defeat in his center would simply drive his army north, back upon its line of supply toward Chattanooga, but that a defeat in the north would cut his army off from its base and cast it adrift in mortal peril in the barren mountain fastnesses to the south. Hence, he had said determinedly that he would continue to support Thomas' position on the left even "if he has to be reinforced by the entire army." Thus, in mid-morning, he ordered Van Cleve's two remaining brigades from his central reserve to go northward to join their brother brigade on Thomas' front. And he took the additional precaution of alerting McCook to prepare his men for a fast movement to the left "at a moment's warning." Then, a half-hour later, Old Rosy told McCook to immediately send two of Phil Sheridan's brigades to the north, contract his frontage so that it could be held by Davis' division alone, and then send Sheridan's remaining brigade northward, too. Thus, Rosecrans was

badly overreacting both to his own fears for his left and the understandable but unjustifiable importunities of an excellent commander whose soldiers were bearing the entire burden of the battle. So Rosecrans fully intended to deploy eight of his divisions on Thomas' front, leaving only two—one of Crittenden's and one of McCook's—divisions in his now shriveled center. He had no fears for his right—southern—flank, and thought himself strong enough in the center to hold frontally with two divisions, since the Confederates were apparently concentrating against his vital left. Indeed, even after sending most of his troops to his left, he was still trying to determine where he could scrape up a few more brigades to send to Thomas in case of need.

By now, of course, Thomas was thoroughly in control of the battlefield on the left. The Rebels were fought to a standstill and he needed no help. Ironically, Rosecrans did not know this. And then Old Rosy received most disquieting news. Two of Thomas' messengers, in passing down the Union lines, had failed to see John Brannan's two brigades posted south of Reynolds' division because—as we have seen—they had sought the better concealment of a cluster of dense woodland. They saw Reynolds' men, and well to the south, the brigades of Wood, who had earlier supplanted Negley's men, allowing them to go north to Thomas; but they could not see Brannan's troops, and so assumed that there was a big gap, what one of Thomas' couriers excitedly called "a chasm, in the center" of the Union line. The meticulous Rosecrans was stunned. How could such a thing occur? The answer, of course, was that it had not occurred! But Old Rosy, with the sudden panic of the overly methodical man discovering that he has not, as he thought and intended, in the end protected himself from each and any dangerous contingency, did not pause—as he should have—to ascertain this. Fearful that the foe would promptly find and exploit this alleged gap in his lines, he did not order a reconnaissance of the area, but moved directly to seal the opening. Thus, he had a staff officer, Maj. Frank S. Bond, draft the following order to Tom Wood: "The general commanding directs that you close up on Reynolds as fast as possible, and support him." There was no gap in the Union line at the moment, but thanks to this message, there very soon would be one.

To Wood, the order did not make sense, as indeed to anyone with a complete knowledge of the actual situation it would not. He could not

Thomas J. Wood led the First Division of Crittenden's corps at Chickamauga. Obeying the order which pulled his troops out of the line of battle, he left a massive hole in the Union Army's defense. The most capable Confederate commander on the field, James Longstreet, discovered and exploited the gap, thus routing the entire right flank of the Army of the Cumberland.

"close up on Reynolds" directly because Brannan's men were between the two divisions. The only thing that he could do to carry out the strange directive was to pull his brigades out of the line and march them north, across the rear of Brannan's units, and thus link up with Reynolds' outfit. It was an unusually awkward procedure, and its implementation would leave a quarter-mile gap of vacated breastworks in the very center of the Union line. Wood thought that the order could not be right. Yet the fact that it did not come to him, as it normally would, from his corps commander, Crittenden, but instead directly from the commanding general, seemed to indicate its special urgency. He discussed it with McCook, who was up front bringing Davis' division in line on Wood's right, so that all of Sheridan's brigades could go northward to join Thomas. The amiable McCook helpfully told the worried Wood that he would simply sidle Davis' division still further to the left to plug the gap that the departure of Wood's units would leave in the army's line. Besides, after his earlier abuse at the hands of Rosecrans for alleged failure to obey orders promptly, Wood had no heart to challenge one of Old Rosy's direct orders, no matter how wrongheaded he sensed that it was. Wood got his men in motion, and then rode ahead to find Reynolds.

Wood instead encountered Thomas. Thomas was surprised. Why send support to Reynolds? Reynolds did not need support; he and Brannan had readily defeated the Rebel thrust at their front. But Thomas, like any commander under pressure, was as avid to increase his supply of troops as a miser is to amass pieces of gold—whether they are needed or not. God, acting through the unknown agency of Rosecrans' confusion, unexpectedly had sent him another full division of combat troops. He did not need them on Reynolds' front, but he reckoned that his northern flank, out beyond Baird's men and the improvised, ragtag line of disparate brigades stretching out to the north and the west, certainly could use help. Wood agreed that he would march his division up to the extreme left of the army's line, provided that Thomas would accept full responsibility for altering his orders from the commanding general. Wily, pragmatic George Thomas must have found it difficult to stifle a smile, as he agreed to do so; he would gladly trade a note for a combat division on any day that God ever made.

Meanwhile, in the Rebel lines, prideful Ol' Pete Longstreet was vexed by this Western army's bungled tactics. He saw that Bragg's piecemeal attacks lacked depth and were doomed to fail. So he sent a note to his invisible chief that he wished to deploy his units not in extended, thin lines, but massed in deep columns on a short front. By now Bragg had grown increasingly impatient with Polk's spasmodic movements, and had sent a staff officer forward to hurry the long, rolling tide of the Confederate assault along. The aide found Stewart, and without consulting Longstreet, ordered his division to attack in yet another disjoined, unsupported assault that, as we have seen, met with defeat.

Old Peter was by now utterly disgusted. Bragg's tactics seemed to him to have disintegrated into a series of frenetic, uncoordinated charges. He would not have any of it in his wing of the army. It was too late to save Stewart's men, but he did not intend to use up any more of his fine infantry in such clumsy, futile efforts. He rode forward immediately to find lean, pugnacious Hood and hold him back.

Hood had Evander Law's and Bushrod Johnson's divisions tightly deployed, and ready to go. Longstreet told Hood to wait. Brig. Gen. Joseph P. Kershaw's division moved up, and Longstreet deployed it behind Law's men. Tom Hindman's division was tucked in at an angle behind Johnson's units. Stewart's embattled division was out beyond Hood's right—northern—flank, and on the so far virgin Hindman's left was the reserve division of Brig. Gen. William Preston, who had led Breckinridge's orphans in their desperate, futile charge on the east bank of Stones River. Thus, Old Peter had deployed four of his six divisions—eleven of his 17 brigades—about 16,000 of his approximately 25,000 troops, on a narrow front of about half a mile. Longstreet had supreme faith in success. With the jaunty confidence of the Virginia army, he had earlier told Hood that "we will of course whip and drive" the Yankees from the battlefield; for this the Army of Northern Virginia almost always did. Hood had experienced the same sensation that Harvey Hill had had when he first joined this odd Western army, where the officers were willing to fight but did not expect to win. To Hood, Longstreet "was the first general I had met since my arrival who talked of victory." And now Old Peter was about to show why.

Longstreet's massed divisions struck the weakest part of the Yankee line a shattering blow shortly before noon. Bushrod Johnson's division was in the lead. In ten minutes, they surged across the dusty LaFayette Road, en-

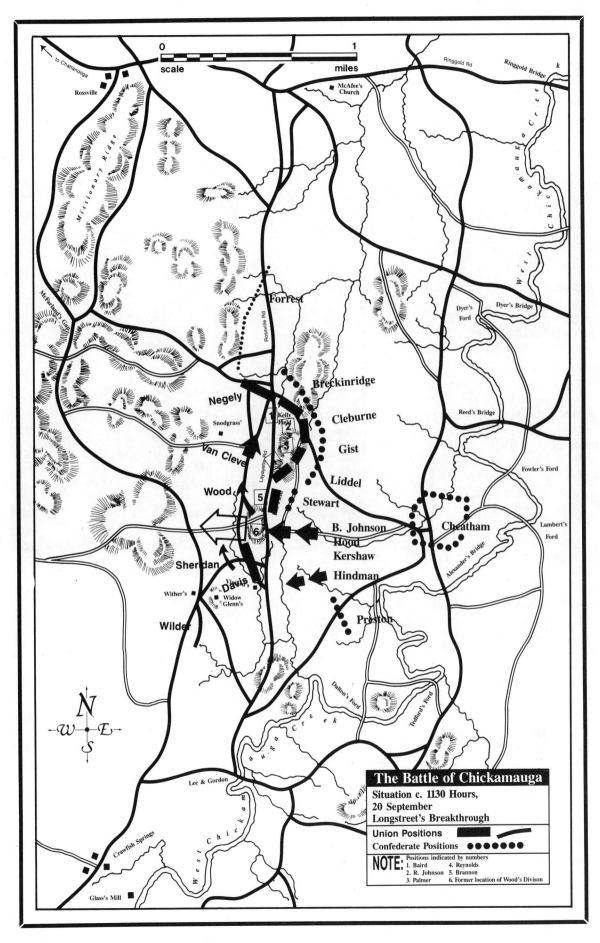

The Battle of Chickamauga

Situation c. 1130 Hours,
20 September
Longstreet's Breakthrough

Union Positions ▬▬▬ ▬▬
Confederate Positions ●●●●●●●

NOTE: Positions indicated by numbers
1. Baird   4. Reynolds
2. R. Johnson   5. Brannon
3. Palmer   6. Former location of Wood's Division

James Longstreet (1821–1904)

James Longstreet, one of Lee's most able lieutenants.

A native of South Carolina, Longstreet graduated West Point 54th out of 62 in the class of 1842. He served in the infantry against the Seminoles, with distinction in Mexico (one wound, two brevets), on the frontier, and in garrison until resigning on 1 June 1861 as a paymaster major. He immediately sought appointment in Confederate service and was made a brigadier general, leading a brigade at Bull Run the following month. That October he was promoted to major general and given a division, which he led with distinction in the opening phases of the Peninsular Campaign in early 1862. He performed poorly when given a higher command shortly thereafter, but redeemed himself during the Seven Days Battles and was ever after in Lee's confidence, commanding the I Corps. He led his corps during the Second Bull Run and Antietam Campaigns, was promoted lieutenant general and commanded his corps at Fredericksburg. In early 1862 the corps served briefly on the Carolina coasts, returning to Virginia in time for the Gettysburg Campaign, about the wisdom of which he had serious reservations. During the Battle of Gettysburg, Longstreet's corps bore the burden of the fighting, particularly on 2 and 3 July. Longstreet was notably dissatisfied with Lee's offensive plans for both days, and his doubts have tended to be confirmed in retrospect. After Gettysburg, Longstreet took his corps west in September of 1863 to support Braxton Bragg's operations and he was largely responsible for the Confederate victory at Chickamauga. Returning to Virginia in early 1864, he was seriously wounded by his own men at the Wilderness in May, not returning to duty until October. He then led his corps and participated in all the succeeding battles of the Army of Northern Virginia from the Wilderness to Appomattox, where he was the only general officer to urge continued resistance if the terms offered by Grant were dishonorable. After the war Longstreet settled in New Orleans, where he became a Republican and a supporter of Reconstruction, once commanding black militiamen against a rioting white mob. This resulted in a vicious campaign to smear his reputation, led most notably by Jubal Early and William Nelson Pendleton, who attempted to place on him all blame for the reverse at Gettysburg. Despite the numerous charges, he retained Lee's confidence to the end. He afterwards was made minister to Turkey by President Grant, who became a close friend, wrote his memoirs, and served in a variety of other government posts. Nicknamed "Old Pete" by the troops and "Old War Horse" by Lee, Longstreet was an excellent corps commander, with a good eye for ground and a fine tactician, whose reputation was long in recovering from the attacks of his enemies.

countering only a little light fire from Brannan's southernmost brigade, to the north, and Davis' northernmost brigade, to the south. Soon Law's division engaged Brannan's well sited units in a hot, bitter firefight, and over on the Confederate left, Hindman's division fought at last, attacking Davis' blue-clad infantry. Nothing was in front of Johnson's men and they received little fire as they climbed over Wood's deserted breastworks, thankful that the formidable Yankee positions were not manned. Then, suddenly, there, right ahead of them, Johnson's men found the last of Wood's brigades, an extended, vulnerable blue column about to march north and rejoin their brethren moving to the far north of Thomas' line. Whooping and yelling, Johnson's brigades struck the long Yankee brigade on both of its exposed flanks and sent its men scattering in all

directions at one and the same time. Johnson's men pushed on through some woods and entered a large clearing. They had advanced half a mile, and had smashed through the Union army's line. They paused to catch their breath and reform their lines.

On a low ridge about a half-mile further west, Yankee guns were deployed, firing northeast and southeast. Some of these guns began to take Johnson's men under fire. Still highly charged with adrenalin, Johnson's men pressed on. He later captured some of the elation of this hitherto luckless army in his report, writing, "The scene now presented was unspeakably grand. The resolute and impetuous charge, the rush of our heavy columns sweeping out from the shadow and gloom of the forest into the open fields flooded with sunlight, the glitter of

Alexander McCook and staff. After the Confederates broke the center of the Union Army, McCook's corps on the right was also swept up in a panicky retreat.

arms . . . of artillery and mounted men, the retreat of the foe, the shouts of . . . our army, the dust, the smoke, the noise . . . of whistling balls and grapeshot and of bursting shell—made up a battle scene of unsurpassed grandeur."

Fair-bearded Hood rode up, holding the reins in one hand, with one arm hanging useless in a sling; as ever aggressive, he shouted at Johnson, "Go ahead, and keep ahead of everything." Johnson's men stormed forward anew, overrunning the Yankee artillery, and advancing another half-mile.

Meanwhile, Tom Hindman's men were rapidly making up for their hitherto listless endeavors as part of the Army of Tennessee. Hindman's troops had the great good fortune to catch their Yankee prey in motion, and thus most vulnerable. Sheridan's two lead brigades were marching north in accordance with Rosecrans' misguided instructions for them to go to the support of Thomas, while Davis' three brigades, which the Rebels had smashed through the day before, were shifting northward to seal the gap created by Wood's disastrous removal from the line. The screaming, surging Rebels struck Davis' units so unexpectedly that the blueclad infantry once again disintegrated; Davis' men rushed headlong for the presumed safety of the rear, many of them stampeding through Sheridan's brigades, making it difficult for the latter to fight and also infecting some of Sheridan's men with the plague of their own panic. Struck then by the charging, whooping Confederate infantry, Sheridan's men fled westward too. An Illinois infantry colonel later noted disgustedly, "McCook's corps was wiped off the field without any attempt at real resistance." The large, volunteer armies of the Civil War were fragile and enigmatic entities. In assault, they could withstand huge slaughter and still keep advancing, and in defense they could resist with dogged stoutness. But adverse and sudden battlefield surprise was more than their volunteer psychology and weak links of command and control could bear; when unexpected disaster impended, they blamed their officers, temporarily excused themselves from a lost cause—as they would individualistically elect to fight hard on other days, when the chances of success were fairer—and flee the battlefield in

On the second day of battle, Lee and Gordon's Mills served as the anchor of the right wing of battle. The Federals of the right had been spared the brunt of the Confederate attack until the second day when Longstreet drove Crittenden's XXI and McCook's XX Corps from the field.

panic.

And that is what transpired on the second day of Chickamauga, as Rosecran's army "voted with its feet." The center of the Union army fled westward and northward, an individualistic, blueclad mob, a vast floodtide of panic that surged across the valley, increasing in frenzied momentum as it swept more and more men and more and more units into its maelstrom. Negley tried to take his last brigade up to join Thomas, but was blocked by the deep thrust of Bushrod Johnson's men, and he too joined the fearful tide of spooked men. Amiable McCook tramped along depressed, aware that his corps had now been routed in three straight big battles, and that this must mean the doom of his career. Crittenden, Davis, even fighting Phil Sheridan, and other men still willing to stand and fight, were swept up in the frenetic torrent, as one man wrote, "like flecks of foam upon a river."

Rosecrans was sitting on his horse in the rear of Davis' division, contemplating the complex details of reinforcing Thomas, when Longstreet's hard, literally Sunday punch struck, bowling Davis' units frantically out of the way.

Seeing Old Rosy make the Sign of the Cross, one man thought, "If the general is crossing himself, we are in a desperate situation."

The Yankee officers watched, as one of them said, "our lines break and melt away like leaves before the wind." Rosecrans calmly told his staff officers, "If you care to live any longer, get away from here." And as one who was present said simply, ". . . the headquarters around me disappeared."

As Rosecrans rode amidst the fleeing throng of beaten soldiers, his calm became dread; he was understandably greatly depressed, for he knew he would be blamed for the army's defeat and castigated for his personal flight. Worse almost, to a rational, methodical man, who sought to plan for every contingency, he did not know how or why the disaster had occurred; so in his mind, the battle was not merely a defeat, but more like some devastating, inexplicable, sudden natural disaster, seemingly without cause or cure. He brooded silently, unspeakably tired, stunned, dazed; to some, he seemed almost catatonic. When at last he reached Chattanooga, his physical and emotional exhaustion

was such that he was unable to dismount his horse without assistance. One sympathetic observer recalled, "The officers who helped him into the house did not soon forget the terrible look of the brave man, stunned by sudden calamity. In later years I used occasionally to meet Rosecrans, and always felt that I could see the shadow of Chickamauga upon his noble face." The report that was sent from Chattanooga to Washington was the epitaph of Rosecrans' command of the Army of the Cumberland. It said: "Chickamauga is as fatal a name in our history as Bull Run."

But the battle was not over. And not all the Yankees fled. Sheridan's third brigade had been retained as a reserve a little southeast of Rosecrans' headquarters. Its commander Brig. Gen. William H. Lyttle, an Ohio lawyer turned soldier, led his men forward in brave, vain hope of blunting the Rebel onslaught. His men, seeing that they were counterattacking against what looked to be most of the enemy army, were shaky. When Lytle was mortally wounded, his brigade broke up and fled, leaving their dying commander to the victors.

William H. Lytle, commander of the First Brigade of Sheridan's division was a recognized poet. He was killed attempting to rally troops to stem Longstreet's powerful advance.

A much more formidable obstacle was John Wilder's fast-shooting reserve brigade. Wilder threw his men into a furious counterattack against the left flank of Hindman's division, ripping at it with the rapid fire of their repeating carbines. The southernmost Confederate brigade stalled, recoiled, and then, before the glad eyes of the desperate Yankees, fled rearward at the sudden reverse, not stopping until they were safely back east of the Lafayette Road. Longstreet was much too able a tactician to be thrown by so predictable a contingency. He smoothly brought up a brigade of Preston's reserve division, and these newcomers, supported by the now sheepish units that had fled, began to push Wilder's badly outnumbered men grudgingly back. As they retired, they left behind them many bloody, grayclad bodies shattered by their fire.

Meanwhile, on the right—northern—edge of the Confederate breakthrough, John Brannan's men shot from the protection of their little wood at the gray tide rolling past them to the south. Seeing this, Law turned his three brigades northward, and struck directly at Brannan's units. The Yankees divided their fire, some were shooting at Johnson's men to the south, others firing at Law's units advancing on them from the east. The woods, so safe and snug before, now suddenly seemed like a bad place to be. Brannan's men feared that they would very soon be crushed to death between Johnson's and Law's divisions. They fell back in haste, but did not flee. Brannan was able to refuse his line, forming up at right angles to Reynolds' line. Or, as one historian gracefully and graphically put it, "Brannan's line swung gatelike, hinged on its left at the juncture with Reynolds. . . ."

Law's men surged on to westward, where they suddenly met a brigade of Van Cleve's division which had been tardy in stepping off northward to the aid of Thomas, and was just now starting to move. When Law's yelling, elated men struck them, nearly helpless in marching column, the Bluecoats learned an impressive lesson in the virtues of punctuality, and were promptly scattered rearward. But a little further along on the way north was Wood's second brigade; its men heard the sounds of firing and wild shouting from their immediate rear, to the south. The leader of this brigade, Col. Charles G. Harker, was young but experienced; a 25-year-old West Pointer, he had been in the big fight at Shiloh and in all the fights, big and small, since. He promptly turned his brigade around, formed it up in line, and led his troops in a furious, slashing counterattack against the northernmost of Law's units. The Texas brigade on Law's exposed right flank was stunned by the sudden storm of fire from Harker's men. The Yankees surged forward, an unexpected grim Blue tide from nowhere. The Texans wavered, then fell back. As the realistic Texans drolly said of themselves, and by implication all of the volunteer soldiers of the Civil War, they fought "like blue blazes when told to," and ran "like a wild turkey when" they knew they were "whipped." Its flank naked to the fire of Harker's aggressive units, Law's division slowed, then stopped its advance.

At this point, John Bell Hood rode up to see the dismal sight of his beloved Texans in full retreat. He galloped one-armed among them, yelling for them to stand and fight. When a Yankee minie ball slashed into Hood's thigh, he fell from his horse into the arms of nearby Texans. Delirious, in shock, he kept repeating what he had earlier told Bushrod Johnson's men, "Go ahead, and keep ahead of everything."

The mournful Texans, anxious to avenge Hood, pulled themselves together and went back into the fight. Meanwhile, Kershaw brought up two brigades of his division, and abetted by the Texans, they drove Harker's tough Yankees back.

But just a little further north, the frayed right—southern—end of Thomas' line still held with grim solidity. The intense fire of Reynolds' determined troops, abetted by a fierce box barrage poured out by the able Federal field artillery, drove Stewart's dogged, torn units back anew. So Thomas held. But a full third of the *Army of the Cumberland* had evaporated. Thus Thomas and his men were alone, surrounded on a hostile battlefield by a swarm of victorious, grayclad infantry. Nonetheless Thomas intended to hold.

As is the way sometimes in combat, the Confederates were confused by the rapidity and extent of their success, so unexpected it was to all save Longstreet. They had achieved a breakthrough; but what to do next? The breakthrough had been accomplished in the wrong place.

Bragg's design was that Polk's wing should achieve the breakthrough, driving the Yankees southward, away from their base at Chattanooga; Longstreet's division were then to have advanced, pushing the enemy before them, then pivot and swing southward, their right units linking up with the left units of Polk's wing to continue driving the Yankees south to their destruction in the wild, empty mountain coun-try. But Polk's wing had failed to breakthrough while Longstreet's wing had succeeded. Clearly, to turn south made no sense now, for there were no Yankees to be found in that direction. And it seemed futile to Longstreet to keep pushing his divisions westward to capture the remnants of the third of Rosecrans' army that was already defeated; they were inevitably doomed anyway if the remaining two-thirds of the Yankee army to the north could be defeated. So Longstreet duly proposed to reverse Bragg's original plan to bring it into accord with the changed tactical situation; he intended to swing his wing of the army to the right—northward—instead of to the left, and drive in the southern flank of the Yankee army while Polk's divisions assaulted it frontally, from the east.

Longstreet was jubilant, not only at what he had already accomplished, but more at what he still expected to accomplish—that rarest of Civil War feats, a crushing, decisive battle of destruction. The enemy he said chipperly, ". . . have fought their last man, and he is running." Old Peter wanted to move in for the kill.

Charles G. Harker, leader of Wood's Third Brigade attempted to maintain a stand against Hood's Texans during the Federal rout, but was outflanked and forced to withdraw.

The imperturbable Virginian George H. Thomas directs a gallant defense on Snodgrass Hill against Longstreet's onrushing troops. The only Union corps commander to stay on the field of battle after the rout of the right flank, Thomas' spirited defense saved the Army of the Cumberland from complete and utter disaster. His actions earned him the title of the Rock of Chickamauga.

But it was no easy matter to switch the axis of advance of so many units. Some divisions had to move great distances in order to get into position for the new attack; Preston's brigades, furthest south in the Confederate line, had to move three miles northward. All of the divisions had their component units mixed up due to the differing degrees of opposition they had met as well as the difficulties of making a long advance over broken, rough terrain. Orders had to be composed and delivered to the proper units; ammunition had to be replenished. And the men wanted to eat. They dined on the usual Nassau—"nausea", the men called it—bacon and sweet potatoes; the Virginians, unused to the potatoes, deemed them a great luxury. All this took time.

Longstreet used some of the time to confer with Bragg. The jubilant Georgian was surprised to find Bragg sad and moody. He discovered that Bragg considered the battle not a victory, but a defeat; his plan to roll up the Union left had failed and he bitterly blamed Bishop Polk for that failure. Longstreet explained his decision to turn his wing northward against the Union right flank. Bragg merely listened gloomily and listlessly. Then Longstreet came to the major point of his visit. He asked Bragg for some of Polk's troops to strengthen the force of his impending blow from the south; after all, he reasoned, all that Polk's units would have to do was to contain the Yankees, setting them up for Longstreet's decisive blow—to act the role of anvil to Longstreet's hammer. Longstreet wanted not only to win a decisive victory, but he also wished to make very sure that everyone for evermore would know who had won it. Bragg, who saw no victory at all, refused, bitterly assailing Polk and his troops, saying: "There is not a man in the right wing who has any fight in him." Bragg then divorced himself from the conduct of the battle once his original plans went awry. His rigidity and indecisiveness rendered him temperamentally unsuited to manage the direction of a fluid battle. He had clung for days to his original plan; when it failed, he had no other, indeed, wished no other.

Yet Braxton Bragg still had a grand opportunity to destroy the *Army of the Cumberland*. However, he lacked the imagination and tactical dexterity to see and seize it. He should have made certain, as so far he had failed to do, that the Union army's line of retreat was blocked prior to carrying out a decisive attack. He should have sent at least one of Polk's battered but still comparatively fresh divisions—they had, after all, certainly made no long advance to tire them out—marching northward behind the rest of the right wing units along the good road to Dyer's Bridge, from there to strike hard westward in an effort to close the Rossville Gap behind the Union army. But Bragg lacked the mental agility and personal flexibility to conceive of such a large stroke, and he lacked the tactical ability and the command and control network to carry it out well. So the battle was now up to Longstreet. Yet in his exuberance, and despite being right in so much, Longstreet was dead, hard wrong—so very, very wrong—about one particularly vital thing: not all the Yankees were running. Indeed, most of them were not even thinking of running.

George Thomas had fought in two wars, and he knew what it was to be forced to retreat; what he did not know was of this thing running. In the Mexican War, as a young gunner, Thomas and his crew had taken their gun down a narrow alley in order to fire at an enemy barricade, but the defensive fire from the rooftops proved too much, and he was ordered to retreat. Thomas would not fall back until he had his men reload and fire one last round at the enemy. Even then, he hated to give ground. Thomas—and therefore Thomas' men—did not run from any battlefield. Thomas and his men had held all day. George Henry Thomas and his men fully intended to continue to hold. And Old Peter Longstreet, and perforce, his triumphant men as well, would soon find this out. For "Old Pap" Thomas and his men intended to hold. It would take a powerful amount of killing to make them run. For Thomas and his men intended to hold.

George Henry Thomas was a man of many nicknames, and a deceptively complex, old professional soldier of the Regular Army. A Virginian, his West Point oath and long army service in a variety of places, some of which became part of the United States, imbued him with a sense of nationalism in an age of sectionalism; so unlike many of Virginia's great soldiers, he remained in the United States Army at the outbreak of the Civil War. Thomas had so many nicknames because his soldiers loved him. And they had good reason to.

Thomas was a deliberate, tenacious man, and thus a deliberate, tenacious fighter. He was a big man, and as one who remembered him recalled, "square everywhere—square face, square shoulders, square step"; he had "blue eyes with depths in them . . . beneath a pent-house of a brow . . . and the whole giving the idea of mas-

George H. Thomas (1816–1870)

A native Virginian, Thomas graduated twelfth in the West Point Class of 1840, entering the artillery. He fought the Seminoles, served on the frontier and in garrison, won two brevets in Mexico, and taught at West Point. During the Secession Crisis he was recuperatng from an arrow wound in the face. Expected to "go south" with his native Virginia, Thomas remained loyal to the Union and by August of 1861 had risen from major to brigadier general. His career during the Civil War was one of considerable brilliance. He served in the Shenandoah Valley in 1861 and then went to Kentucky (Mill Springs, 19–20 January 1862). Appointed a major general in April of '62, he commanded divisions and later corps in all the principal battles in Tennessee. At Chickamauga the heroic stand of his troops earned him the nickname "The Rock of Chickamauga" and subsequently command of the *Army of the Cumberland* when Grant assumed direction of affairs in Central Tennessee. His troops again distinguished themselves at Missionary Ridge and Thomas thereafter became one of the principal Federal commanders, serving under Sherman during the Atlanta Campaign (Peach Tree Creek, 20 July '64). When Hood, unable to stop Sherman directly, invaded Tennessee in an effort to draw him away from central Georgia, Thomas stopped him cold at Nashville (15–16 December '64), despite unfamiliar, mistrustful subordinates. After the war Thomas continued in the service, dying in San Francisco, where he was serving as commanding general for the West Coast. A big, deliberate man of considerable ability, Thomas' Virginia background probably retarded his rise to independent command.

George H. Thomas, known to his men as "Pap" or "Old Slow Trot," was one of the Union Army's most brilliant corps commanders. A Virginian who stayed loyal to the Union, he could conduct an almost indestructable defense on the battlefield, as he proved at Chickamauga. Later he led his troops to take Missionary Ridge, marched with Sherman on Atlanta, and annihilated J.B. Hood's army at Nashville.

sive solidity. . . ." Steady, slow, massive, solid—and unmovable when he did not want to be moved.

A father figure to them, he was called "Old Pap" by his men. In the Old Army he was called "Old Slow-Trot," for he had injured his spine in an accident and to ride his horse fast hurt him, and because the nomenclature seemed apt to his slow, methodical ways. He just called himself, "Slow."

Thomas was chary of the lives of his men. He fully understood the defensive firepower of the rifle, and he did not like to waste his infantry in hasty, heedless, desperate assaults against strong defenses; when possible, he made his men build strong defenses out of trees and dirt in order to maximize their own defensive firepower. But, unlike many prudent and methodical soldiers, Thomas was not timid in battle. He did not fear battle. He simply coveted battle on his own terms—the terms most favorable to his men. His men understood this. And so they loved and trusted him; they followed him willingly wherever he led. Thomas was a counter-puncher. His preference was to to fight defensively, to utilize strong field works and the defensive firepower of the rifle to inflict heavy losses on an enemy attacking in the open and then smash the weakened foe with a pulverizing counterattack by his largely intact force. Some of the great commanders of history used similar methods; Wellington was a counter-puncher, so was Erwin Rommel—but, unlike Thomas, none accused those redoubtable gentlemen of being too slow.

So now, on the afternoon of the second day at Chickamauga, George Henry Thomas, six feet tall, over two hundred pounds—a big man for his times, and in more ways than one—was left to command the chaos of a disintegrating army in a lost battle, alone, tenacious, imperturbable, unruffled.

Brannan's units had swung back from the Confederate onslaught to form a new line on the rising ground to the right rear of Reynolds' division, holding Thomas' right flank. Yet Brannan had set up a little north of Reynolds' line, so that there was a diagonal gap between Brannan's left and Reynolds' right. Single brigades from the shattered commands of Wood, Negley, and Van Cleve joined Brannan's men to try to hold the east-west segment of the new line. The original north-south line, bent inward on both flanks, was still held by the divisions of Baird, Johnson, Palmer, and Reynolds. Thomas now took a brigade each from Johnson and Palmer, and sent them to support Brannan. Brannan's position was densely wooded, and the Rebels would have to move uphill to attack it. It was good defensive ground, but it was held by men from different units, many of whom had already been beaten once by the enemy. Thomas did not know a lot of them; but he sensed that they were shaky.

So Thomas rode over—slowly—to steady them. As one historian wrote, "A big man, George Thomas . . . easy to spot on his charger . . . riding where the rank and file could not miss seeing him—or feeling his eyes on them. Cool, completely unflurried. . . . Soldiers . . . steadied. . . ." He rode up to tough Charles Harker and told him, "This hill must be held and I trust you to do it." Harker said grimly, "We will hold it or die here." Thomas rode a little down the line, and came up to an Ohio officer in Harker's outfit. "This point must be held." The Buckeye colonel looked back hard at him and said, "We will hold this group, or go to heaven from it." Around him, blueclad infantrymen nodded approvingly. Thomas, running his fingers through his gray whiskers—the only outward sign of his inward worry—could only wait and see.

Joe Kershaw's South Carolinians and Mississippians were the first to try the new Yankee line. Kershaw thought the Blue line brittle; one hard blow and it would crack. His men struck hard at its left flank, a little too far west of the gap that extended back from Reynolds' right rear. The two Rebel brigades, struggling uphill, were slashed by heavy fire from the rifles of Harker's brigade, on Brannan's left, and of that of Brig. Gen. William Hazen, brought over from Palmer's division; bloodied and surprised, they fell back. Twice more, Kershaw sent his men up that wooded slope; and again and again, they were shot to pieces by the torrent of Yankee fire. Finally, he gave it up. Kershaw watched his beaten men, sprawled winded, "panting like dogs" from their exertion, wide-eyed, faces shiny and gray from sweat and fear, and hoped that at least his attacks had forced the enemy to shift reserves to this part of the line, for he knew his attack was but the first of Longstreet's blows.

In the woods far to the Rebel left, at the extreme right of the new Federal east-west line, two victorious Confederate divisions, under Bushrod Johnson and Tom Hindman, were massing so as to overlap the end of the Union front and smash in the entire right rear of Thomas' corps. Since the Federals were deployed facing south and east and this assault would come

from the southwest, if that happened few of Thomas' men would escape. And there was nothing, it seemed, to prevent it from happening. Yet something did. That something, significant not for the first time this day, was the greater initiative of the Union officers.

Four miles away to the north, tough, profane, aggressive Maj. Gen Gordon Granger, a hard-bitten Old Regular waited restlessly with his small *Reserve Corps* posted to block the main road to Chattanooga. He was a hard, curt man with much of the loner in him, short with his

fellow officers, and not beloved of his men because of his rigid, harsh methods of training and discipline. Granger could hear the peal of church bells in the peaceful city behind him; but ahead of him he apprehensively heard more ominous sounds, the muffled booming of artillery. He reason that he was hearing the sounds of an intense battle on Thomas' front. Thomas must need him. Why were there no orders to go in? Granger was at best not a patient man, and now, knowing that fellow soldiers needed his help, and maybe needed it in a hurry, he grew

The headquarters of Gordon Granger, commander of the Army of the Cumberland reserve corps. From here, Granger ordered his troops to reinforce Thomas at a critical moment.

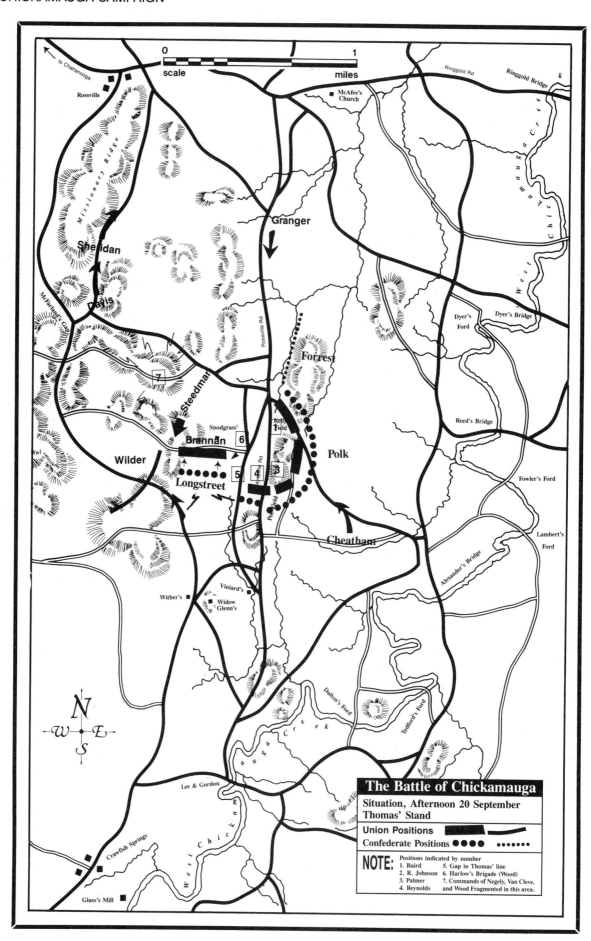

to Chattanooga

Rossville

McAfee's Church

Ringgold Rd

Ringgold Bridge

Missionary Ridge

Granger

Sheridan

McFarland's Gap

Davis

Rossville Rd

Forrest

Dyer's Ford

Dyer's Bridge

Steedman

7

Snodgrass'

Kelly Field

Reed's Bridge

Brannan

6

Polk

Wilder

5

4

Longstreet

Poe Field

Fowler's Ford

Cheatham

Lambert's Ford

Alexander's Bridge

Viniard's

Wither's

Widow Glenn's

N
W — E
S

Dalton's Ford

Tedford's Ford

Chickamauga Creek

West Chickamauga

Lee & Gordon

The Battle of Chickamauga

Situation, Afternoon 20 September
Thomas' Stand

Union Positions ▬▬▬▬ ▬▬▬

Confederate Positions ●●●● ·······

NOTE: Positions indicated by number
1. Baird   5. Gap in Thomas' line
2. R. Johnson   6. Harlow's Brigade (Wood)
3. Palmer   7. Commands of Negely, Van Cleve,
4. Reynolds   and Wood Fragmented in this area.

Crawfish Springs

West Chickamauga

Glass's Mill

more and more restive at his enforced idleness. Pointing off to the southeast, he told his chief of staff, "Why the hell does Rosecrans keep me here? . . . There is the battle." He got no answer. And more time passed.

Finally, Granger climbed up a haystack and stared hard through his field glasses, like many a soldier before and after him, fated to wait in ignorance, seemingly alone and forgotten in the midst of an epic battle, not knowing what is happening beyond their ken to determine their destiny; but, like all such, Granger was thwarted. The densely wooded terrain blocked his view. Disgustedly, he slammed his field glasses back in their case, and slid down the haystack, cursing. Then he made up his mind. "I am going to Thomas, orders or no orders!" As was his duty, his chief of staff reminded him, "And if you go, it may bring disaster to the army and to you a courtmartial." These were powerful arguments to a long-service Regular, bred to obedience and constancy. But the dispersal of the peacetime army in small frontier-defense units, so pernicious an influence in most respects, was a boon in one way. It encouraged men, long isolated from the advice of superiors, to rely on their own judgment. Gordon Granger had long ago learned to trust his own soldierly instincts in tight places; and now he was prepared to do so once again. Granger replied, "There's nothing in our front. . . . Don't you see Bragg is piling his whole army on Thomas? I am going to his assistance." And he did, leading forward two brigades immediately under brave, bluff Brig. Gen. James B. Steedman, leaving one in reserve to hold the Rossville Gap.

The day was now hot, and Steedman's men plodded down the LaFayette Road, churning up ankle-deep dust in thick, choking, sallow brown clouds, glancing up anxiously ahead of them in the direction of the ominous thunder towards which they were marching. Then, about a mile down the road, they came under fire—the flash and screech and boom of two batteries of Confederate horse artillery. These Rebel cavalry and gunners were screening Polk's north flank. Steedman had to halt his southward-marching column, and then redeploy his men in battle lines advancing eastward. The blueclad infantry easily overlapped the flanks of the tenacious, but heavily outnumbered, Rebel gunners and their supporting troopers and forced them back. But as soon as Steedman's soldiers had resumed their line of march, the Rebels reappeared and commenced firing anew. Disgustedly, Granger realized that this grim, time-consuming ballet of

Gordon Granger, without orders, commanded his troops to support Thomas who was hard pressed by Longstreet's Confederates. Granger's reinforcements saved the day for the Union troops on Snodgrass Hill, as well as the Army of the Cumberland.

expert delaying tactics could go on for hours, and resolutely cut it short by casting aside the last remnant of his obedience to Rosecrans' orders. He ordered his third brigade down the LaFayette Road, too, thus leaving Rossville Gap open. He was now not merely compromising his orders; he was disobeying them—a hard thing, indeed, for a Regular soldier infamous for his strict discipline. He knew that if things went badly this day, his career would be ruined. Yet he also knew that fellow soldiers desperately needed help; and in order to help them, he had to disobey orders. Besides, he must also have reasoned, if things did indeed go very badly this day, he might very well have even more formidable worries than merely a prematurely ended career. Granger took his men off the road, moving southwest through the woods and fields, bypassing the Rebels and leaving them for his last brigade to contain. He was in a hurry; there were comrades up ahead who needed help.

Thomas saw Granger's men coming—and thought they were Rebels descending upon his open northern flank. He was contemplating how to reckon with this new disaster when something about the gait of these approaching soldiers told him that they were not fresh assailants, but men moving up to reinforce him. Granger soon reached him and shook hands; Thomas smiled broadly at this hard, unpopular officer he was now so glad to see.

William Preston, Confederate division commander at Chickamauga.

Johnson's and Hindman's Rebel infantrymen were just moving out of the cover of the woods, ready to overlap and overwhelm the Union right flank; steadily they climbed the low, forested ridge just south of the end of the Federal line. Thomas and Granger, two old soldiers with common instincts, looked up, and both knew what had to be done. Granger pointed at the lines of Confederate infantry, "Those men must be driven back." Thomas nodded and said, "Can you do it?" Gordon Granger had trained his young Midwestern infantrymen hard and relentlessly; they were not Regulars, but he knew they would fight hard. He nodded back at Thomas, and said in his terse, hard-bitten way, "Yes. My men are fresh, and they are just the fellows for that work. They are raw troops and they don't know any better than to charge up there."

Steedman, a big, broad, bluff man, stout-hearted and possessed of plenty of common sense, told a staff officer to make sure that his name was spelled correctly in the newspaper obituaries, and promptly spurred his horse forward and called for his men to follow him.

The Union infantry moved forward through the brush and waist-high weeds and trees toward the low hump of ridgeline ahead; then their double lines slowed as they saw the numbers of the enemy and they began to take fire. Artillery rounds burst loudly and redly nearby, then came the zing and crackle of rifle balls. Nearly exhausted from the climb and heat, sweating and frightened, they went down, thinking to rest, to shelter from the fire overhead. Steedman knew that if they stayed down long, he would never get them moving forward

again; they would have had time to decide that they wanted to live another day, and the counterattack would die. He rode forward purposefully, sure that he was a dead man this day, and grabbed the colors of an Illinois infantry regiment, yelling "Forward!" over and over again, and telling his stalled men that if they were too frightened to go forward they could go back—but their flag could not. Steedman's horse was shot, and he tumbled to the ground, hurt by the fall. But he rose and limped forward, swinging the Illinois banner and shouting, "Follow me!"

Tired and scared, wild-eyed and sweaty with fatigue and fear, the Midwesterners rose and followed Steedman into the storm of fire; they fired themselves as they ran forward, more to help their own morale than in hopes of hitting much. But they kept running forward, ignoring those falling in their midst, blindly and single-mindedly. They did not falter again. They overwhelmed the surprised Rebels by the violent, implacable impetus of their charge. They broke the Rebels and drove them back; then they beat a hasty counterattack. It all took twenty minutes, and it cost them one-fifth of their number, but Gordon Granger's men, as their rough boss had somehow understood that they would, had taken the high ground—and had held it.

For the first time that day, "Old Peter" was troubled. The bloody repulse of first Kershaw's men, then Johnson's and Hindman's troops demonstrated that the Yankee infantry was far from done. Indeed, he now saw that they were "full of fight, even . . . aggressive." Hindman, nicked by a little fragment from a Yankee artillery round, grimly concurred, saying that he had "never known Federal troops to fight so well." But then he had never gone up against Old Pap Thomas' boys before.

Moreover, Longstreet was, as ever, a clear-sighted and analytical tactician. The attack had failed, he was sure, because it was not properly coordinated. Kershaw, anxious to bounce the Yankees out of their new line before they made it strong, had acted too hastily, striking before Johnson's and Hindman's troops attacked. What was needed was better coordination, mutually supporting assaults—one hard coordinated blow, not a series of piecemeal attacks. Longstreet ordered Kershaw and Johnson and Hindman to renew their attacks at either end of the new Yankee line; then he brought up Preston's reserve division to hit the Yankee center hard, while Law's division struck between Kershaw's and Preston's men, and Stewart's attacked to the right of Kershaw's units, ever so near the vulnerable but unappreciated little gap in the Yankee front between Reynolds' right and Brannan's left.

A little before 1600 hours William Preston, a courtly, brave Kentuckian, much beloved of his men, sent two of his brigades forward. The Yankees in the center had had a little time in their new positions to improvise defenses with stones and some fallen trees. As soon as Preston's men moved grimly out of the woods and started up the slope, they were lashed and withered by furious gusts of rifle fire. They were able to get to within about eighty yards of the Union lines; then they could move forward no more. But they did not fall back. Instead, they remained standing in the open for a long hour that seemed forever, trading rifle fire with protected defenders. If they were unable to advance they sought to pin the enemy with their fire, so that others might advance. Preston's men were shredded by the Yankee fire, losing in that single, terrible hour, 1054 of their original number of 2,879 attackers. Yet their pressure helped.

Bishop Polk had ordered his divisions to resume their assaults on Thomas' original north-south line. So now the pressure on Thomas' front was complete; he was being attacked all along his extended line—no longer would he be able to move units from quiet sectors to support hard-hit points in the line. Now a breakthrough anywhere along his front would be difficult, if not impossible, to contain, and might well lead to the destruction of his corps, which had fought so well for so long and deserved a better fate.

As Thomas contemplated what to do next, the grim, bitter battle went on around him. And as on the day before, it raged and roared and crackled with an intense, furious, persistent mad momentum seemingly of its own, independent of the will of men. But Thomas' men were running short of ammunition; including casualties, the per-soldier expenditure of ammuniton was more than eighty rounds apiece on this long fierce day of battle. An Ohio infantry regiment, numbering 535 men at the start of the day, fired almost 45,000 rounds of rifle ammunition. The army's ordnance train was gone, disappeared in the disaster to the rest of the line. Granger's men had come south with 95,000 precious rounds, but at the present rate of expenditure, this could not—and did not—last long. The Union troops kept fighting by stripping the nearby dead of their ammunition, and when they called out for more rounds, Thomas grimly, laconically told them, "Use your bay-

The imperious George H. Thomas, coming from a Southern background, was considered suspect by Washington D.C. and military high command. For this reason he was consequently deprived of the promotions and recognitions a man of his ability deserved.

onets." Increasingly along the Union line could be heard a new, ominous sound—the rasp and sharp click of bayonets being pulled from scabbards and affixed to rifles. Thomas' men would not be able to hold on much longer.

Thomas did not want to retreat in daylight, fearing a Rebel pursuit that would destroy his extended, vulnerable retreating columns. But now, at about 1700 hours, with the Rebel pressure increasing all along his front and his ammunition supply menacingly diminished, Thomas feared a Confederate breakthrough of the overextended, outnumbered line, a breakthrough that he now lacked the reserves to contain.

Thomas ordained a withdrawal in sequence, commencing on his left, where the pressure from Bishop Polk's depleted units was less intense than that of Old Pete Longstreet's more peppy units to his right. Reynolds' division would pull back first, then Palmer's, then Johnson's, and then Baird's, which would serve as the rear guard; similarly, the mixed units on the right would then also fall back in sequence. Reynolds' men began moving out at 1730.

Once again the Union army was helped greatly by the initiative of its subordinate commanders. For when Reynolds' brigades reached the northern end of the Union line, prepared to swing west as ordered to move through McFarland's Gap and on toward Rossville and Chattanooga via the Dry Valley Road a little west of Missionary Ridge, they found Confederate infantrymen from Liddell's brigades. After two days of trying, the Rebels had at last found Baird's left flank and were deploying to smash it in. Reynolds unhesitatingly discarded

Officers of the 365th Illinois served in William H. Lytle's brigade at Chickamauga.

Men who fought and died at Chickamauga, soldiers of the 5th Georgia Regiment fought with distinction at Chickamauga, but suffered the largest casualties of the war.

his orders and ordered his brigades to mount a strong counterattack to the north. The fierce charge of Reynolds' desperate men drove the Confederates well back, thus opening the line of retreat for the three divisions following. The Rebel divisions of Breckinridge and fighting Pat Cleburne maintained growing pressure on the three Yankee divisions behind Reynolds, and the Union troops were reluctantly compelled to leave their wounded for the enemy.

On the southern segment of the Union line, the Confederates were able at long last but a little too late, to achieve a breakthrough. When Steedman pulled his men back off the little ridge at the western end of the line—the ridge that they had bled so much to take and hold—Johnson's and Hindman's Rebel soldiers came rushing up over the top in close, fast pursuit. At that point, gentlemanly William Preston sent his reserve brigade into the gap; the fresh Confederates rushed through and swung quickly right—eastward—onto the now exposed flank of the Federal line. Three Yankee regiments were forced to surrender, and this last remnant of Thomas' front collapsed and fled. Yet most of the Union troops from this end of the line made it out to safety.

The Union troops were saved because they marched rapidly, impelled by greater necessity than their pursuers; for them, marching fast to westward meant safety, but to the following Rebels, rapid pursuit meant simply another chance to die after having survived so much already. No one wanted to be the last man killed at Chickamauga. And the Yankees were saved because Reynolds' hard-fighting troops did well in their job as the army's rear guard. Two of Reynolds' Indiana regiments had discovered an abandoned, broken-down ammunition wagon along the line of retreat, and they were able to load up with rifle ammunition. Thomas himself soon passed that way, and noted these well supplied Hoosier infantrymen. He told them that they were the army's rear gaurd. And they made a good job of it, blasting away with dense red volleys of rifle fire at the pursuing shadows back behind them in the deepening night.

And so Thomas' men marched out. They marched out with, as one historian said, "the taste of defeat bitter in their mouths and a great weariness in their limbs." A veteran infantry captain recalled, "Weary, worn, tired and hungry, we sullenly dragged ourselves along, feel-

Officers of the 36th Illinois served in William H. Lytle's brigade at Chickamauga.

Officers of the 36th Illinois. After Chickamauga, these Federals joined George H. Thomas' successful campaign against John B. Hood at Nashville.

ing . . . shame. . . ." Another historian described it thus: "Weary blue columns trudged along a road lined by miles of wounded. . . . Some of them hobbled or crawled along in pitiful efforts to keep up . . . others lay quiet by the roadisde. . . . Darkness descended . . . mingling and mixing the . . . commands in what seemed inextricable confusion."

So Thomas' men marched out—depressed and weary, glad to escape but feeling guilt at the gladness; they saw only that they had been defeated, but they did not see what that had done. They had saved the *Army of the Cumberland*. And they were entitled to march out proud and jaunty. When Old Rosy first heard the news of their

stand, he merely but meaningfully said, "This is good enough. The day isn't lost yet." Thomas' men had saved the *Army of the Cumberland* by standing fast against nearly twice their number. But they did not see that. They marched amid the wreckage and chaos of defeat, and they saw only that. They did not see that they had won, too. And so Old Rosy's brief words were a good epitaph for this beaten-victorious army, an army of mixed feelings, an army too sad to be proud. "This is good enough." Thus Thomas' men marched out.

Thomas withdrew his units up to Rossville Gap, prepared to stand against renewed assaults of the Rebels. But none came.

NO MORE FLANKS

The End of the Battle of Destruction

The goal of the greatest tacticians of military history was the battle of destruction—the Cannae or the Austerlitz—the annihilation of the main enemy field force in a single clash. The example of Napoleon inspired Civil War battle leaders with the possibility of once again attaining rapid, decisive victory in warfare, and so at the outset they made the battle of destruction their objective.

There were two means to achieve the battle of destruction. The first was through a breakthrough of a portion of the enemy front—a penetration, which when exploited, allowed one to concentrate against the severed segments of the foe's line and defeat them in detail. The way to attain a penetration, or breakthrough, was to mass great strength against a portion of the enemy front and attack frontally

with combined arms—using field artillery to suppress enemy fire, a cavalry sweep to disperse enemy fire by forcing the infantry into squares, and a massed infantry bayonet charge to smash forward—while also executing simultaneously a series of smaller but coordinated attacks on other parts of the foe's front in order to pin his reserves tightly in place and prevent them from moving to support

Union battle line as it might appear in combat. In front are skirmishers, soldiers sent to the front to determine weaknesses in the enemy positions. Behind them is the main battle column.

the forces at the main point of attack or to seal off the penetration and prevent its exploitation.

The second method of achieving decisive victory was to outmaneuver the foe—to use mobility and subtlety to find and turn an exposed flank of the enemy line, to roll up the units along the defensive front piecemeal. The flank attack, like the frontal attack, also worked best when supported by lesser but well-coordinated assaults at other points along the enemy front in order to pin reserves and prevent them from moving to contain the main flank assault by setting up a new defensive line in the rear at right angles to the original front, thus transforming the main flank attack into merely another frontal assault.

Such were the theoretical bases of the concept of the battle of destruction—tested and well proven in the campaigns of Napoleon—which Civil War generals wished to implement. But, of course, what no one could then realize—because it would take two years of fierce, bloody combat to demonstrate—was that the theory would no longer work in practice. The armies of the Civil War were very, very different from the armies that fought the Napoleonic Wars; so different that the old tactics could no longer succeed on the battlefield. The Napoleon battle of destruction was unattainable, nothing like it would appear again in warfare until 1940, a product of still newer technologies and vastly different armies.

The transition from the smooth-bore musket of the past to the rifled musket of the Civil War doomed the traditional tactics to bloody futility. The smooth-bore musket was an inaccurate, short-range weapon—its true effective range was on the order of 40-50 yards, and its lack of accuracy did not admit of much aimed fire. It was necessary to resort to volley fire in order to have much chance to inflict serious casualties with musket fire; volume of fire, not individual accuracy, was the key. As always, weaponry dictated tactics. The armies of the age of the smooth-bore musket fought at close range and in tight, compact

masses; they had to fight in this way in order to make their fire effective. These closely massed ranks were also necessary in order to project a solid, continuous line of bayonets to discourage the approach of cavalry, which only had to gallop fifty yards to close, while the infantry reloaded their muskets. These tight, compact formations—little moving forts of flesh and blood—were easy to command and control in a firefight, but exceedingly difficult to maneuver about the battlefield with any speed or flexibility because they had to move very precisely and slowly in order to retain at all times the mass that made them effective. An army composed of such formations could not change front readily nor maneuver rapidly to compensate for any sudden or drastic change in the tactical situation. Tactical leadership was highly professional, thoroughly trained, and usually possessed of much battle experience.

The rifled musket of the American Civil War was a much more accurate weapon, making effective individual, aimed fire possible. The effective range of the rifled musket was nearly ten times as great as that of the old smooth-bore! Battles now had to be fought at correspond-

Zouaves of the 4th Michigan Infantry armed with the common rifled musket used by the Federal soldier.

Members of a Confederate cavalry detachment in the West. At Chickamauga dismounted cavalry troopers fought the Yankees as infantry in the dense woods of the battlefield.

ingly longer range, and by units that could be deployed in much looser formations, as it was no longer necessary to rely upon tight formations to produce accurate fire, and with a longer-range weapon each man could control more ground with fire. These looser formations were much more difficult to exert tight command and control over in a firefight, and it was much harder to coordinate the operations of several such units than it had been in the age of more compact formations. However, the looser formations were much more maneuverable on the battlefield because men could move individually, concerning themselves with speed of movement, rather than precision of movement, since it was no longer necessary for them to move in a concerted mass in order for them to retain effectiveness of fire. These rifle armies composed of looser, more flexible formations were able to move speedily; hence, they could respond to a battle emergency more rapidly and change front more readily than the armies of the past. However, leadership was only partly professional. Many officers were poorly trained due to the nature of the pre-war army's primary duties, and for the most part lacking in direct experience of battle.

In short, the rifle caused a military revolution not only because it increased the range and accuracy of infantry firepower, as is well known, but because it also increased the rate of infantry mobility, which is less well understood. Musket armies maneuvered slowly in close-ordered ranks, pausing often to dress lines to avoid leaving dangerous gaps and lessening the effect of their fire. Rifle armies moved much more quickly, in looser, more flexible lines, heedless of gaps which could be covered by their augmented firepower.

It was this combination of increased defensive firepower and greater mobility of the Civil War armies that doomed the traditional battle of destruction.

The defensive firepower of the rifle made it much harder to achieve a frontal penetration, or breakthrough. First, it diminished and even negated the efficacy of the supporting arms that were supposed to prepare the way for the final infantry frontal assault. Offensive artillery fire was not nearly as effective against the more loosely deployed and partly concealed riflemen as it had been against tightly-packed musketeers. Also, the great range of the rifle enabled well-placed defenders to inflict casualties on rash or aggressive gunners; men with muskets were easily out-ranged by field artillery; riflemen were not.

Offensive cavalry thrusts were doomed by the rifle. Horses were large targets, and now they could be hit at 500 yards instead of fifty. A cavalryman at least had a chance to cover fifty yards while an infantryman with a musket reloaded; he had no chance to cover ten times that distance while a rifleman reloaded. But without a cavalry charge, the firepower of defending infantry could not be dispersed in all-around defense but would continue to be concentrated frontally.

With offensive field artillery reduced in effectiveness, and with cavalry charges impossible, the decisive infantry frontal assault rarely had much chance to succeed in the face of the but little diminished defensive firepower of better protected riflemen shooting at men advancing in the open.

In addition, the poor command and control qualities of both Union and Confederate tactical leadership usually meant that supporting assaults designed to pin the defender's reserves were poorly coordinated and thus were undertaken piecemeal, instead of simultaneously, and so failed to prevent the defender from shifting forces to meet the main assault. This, of course, was one of Bragg's major failings throughout the Chickamauga Campaign. But he

had plenty of company in both armies during the Civil War. George B. McClellan suffered defeat at Antietam (17 September 1862) for the same reason. And so too did a host of other Civil War tacticians, because the new, looser formations necessitated by the advent of the rifle, while much more mobile, were also much less amenable to tight command and control.

The result of this combination of factors was that it became virtually impossible to achieve a frontal penetration, or breakthrough, of a defensive front. Attempts to do so produced litle but tactical stalemate and extremely heavy losses to the infantry.

This trend was duly noted in the first year of war, so intelligent commanders abandoned the direct frontal assault in favor of the more indirect approach of finding and turning the exposed flank of the defensive line. Robert E. Lee and Thomas "Stonewall" Jackson were the masters of this method, as Second Manassas (29 August 1862) and Chancellorsville (2–3 May 1863) attest. Bragg, of course, tried less complex flank attacks throughout the Chickamauga Campaign, but they did not work as he intended because his tactical instincts were fuzzy, his battle management

Federal cavalry troops.

A column of Ohio troops that served in the West. They typify the common Western soldier who fought at Shiloh, Murfreesboro, Chickamauga, and at Missionary Ridge.

By the Civil War more accurate rifles doomed the "romantic" cavalry charge. Mounted troops were thus relegated to other less thrilling duties, such as patrols and reconnaissance.

clumsy, and his command and control of his army nonexistent.

It was noted that this approach often produced victories, but not decisive victories; the flank assaults sometimes forced the enemy to retreat, but even when most successful, they invariably failed to destroy the foe's army. The reasons for this, of course, were the much greater infantry mobility and firepower of the riflemen composing the Civil War armies. The looser, more flexible formations made possible by the rifle made it possible for at least some units to march rapidly to contain the flank assault even in the midst of defeat. The firepower of the better protected defenders allowed them to hold off much larger numbers of attackers. Then the defenders, their numbers increasing, would set up a new defensive line, indeed sometimes—as Thomas' right at Chickamauga—at right angles to the original front, thus transforming the attacker's original flank attack into just another costly frontal attack.

Hence, it was the combination of increased defensive firepower and greater tactical mobility of the infantry—both alike made possible by the transition from the smoothbore musket to the rifled musket as the basic infantry weapon—that put an end to the battle of destruction, and hopes of a rapid, decisive victory in the Civil War.

There were no more flanks: in the age of the rifle, all assaults were frontal assaults in the end.

THE TWELVE-YEAR-OLD BUCK SERGEANT

During the Civil War, it was not unusual for the volunteer regiments in both the Union and Confederate armies to recruit boys as young as ten to serve as drummers. This is the tale of one of them.

In 1861, John Lincoln Clem—"Johnny"—was ten years old. Born to a patriot family, he sought to join the Union army. But Johnny was very small; he was short and weighed only sixty pounds. He tried to enlist in the *22nd Michigan Infantry,* but was rejected as undersized. Then he tried the *3rd Ohio Infantry.* He was turned down once again, this time somewhat ignominiously. The colonel rudely allowed that he "wasn't enlisting infants."

But Johnny Clem was a shrewd and tenacious youngster. He waited until the *22nd Michigan* marched off to war. Then, reckoning that the Wolverines had marched too far to be likely to take the trouble to send him back, he promptly ran away from home to join the regiment. He was right. The Michigan soldiers let him stay. Perhaps it was merely the administrative laxity and loose structure of the amorphous, early-Civil War units that allowed Johnny Clem his chance to "see the elephant," or perhaps it was simply that the young Michigan infantrymen admired his grit, as well they should have!

Johnny Clem became the proud drummer boy of *Company C, 22nd Michigan Infantry.* Ahead were many long marches over dusty roads in stifling heat, as the Wolverines moved fitfully toward their rendezvous with blood and destiny. Sometimes the little, short-

A drummer boy, such as Johnny Clem, in full dress.

legged drummer boy from Company C, face streaked with sweat and dirt, eyes shiny from fatigue, would begin to stagger and wobble in pained weariness. At those times one of the company officers would always dismount, pick Johnny up and swing him into the saddle. Now riding, Johnny would continue to beat the march cadence on the drum slung around his

neck. Since he was not lawfully enrolled in the regiment, he received no pay; so the Company's officers chipped in each month to provide him with a private's pay of thirteen dollars. He was not placed on the Regiment's payroll until May, 1863! By that time, he was a combat veteran.

It was at Shiloh, bloody Shiloh, that Johnny Clem first beat his drum in battle. He heard the loud buzz of swarms of Rebel rifle rounds, and he saw older friends die. His drum was smashed by fragments from a Rebel shell. But he did not mind that too much, because it gave him a chance to fight back. His mates cut down a musket to a size that he could handle, and he joined the killing part of the war. As Johnny said, "I did not like to stand and be shot at without shooting back."

At Chickamauga, the Michiganers tried to keep Johnny back with the gunners where he would be a little safer. But Johnny knew he lacked the size and strength to be of use as an artilleryman. So when his battery moved up toward the firing, Johnny picked up his undersized musket and left his caisson, hurrying forward to help out his outfit in a tough fight. Then things began to happen fast, as they sometimes will in combat.

A Rebel officer on horseback, saber raised, galloped toward him and shouted for him to surrender. Johnny aimed quickly and fired, blasting the man off his horse. Then Johnny continued to move forward. But soon he was hit—a shell fragment in the hip—and he went down. The Rebels were winning now; the Bluecoats still able were being driven back. Johnny was captured. The Rebels had caught a minnow. But not for long.

The Rebels assembled their bag of Yankee prisoners and herded them through the trees and brush toward the rear. At an opportune moment, Johnny ducked away into a patch of tall grass. He played dead for hours until he felt safe enough to move back to the Union lines. While hospitalized for his wound, he was promoted to lance sergeant. He was twelve years old. As one writer said, "Think of a sixty-three-pound sergeant . . ."

Johnny Clem's story caught the fancy of the people of those harder yet more sentimental times, and he became a minor celebrity of the war. Chicago ladies sent him a fine, new uniform, and pretty Kate Chase, daughter of the Secretary of the Treasury, presented him with a silver medal. Then Lance Sergeant John Lincoln Clem went back to the grim, bloody war in the West.

John rode dispatches for Pap Thomas, and in the Atlanta campaign, his pony was killed by Rebel fire, and he received his second wound of the war when a Reb round mangled one of his ears.

After the war, John sought to enter West Point in order to become an officer; but he clearly did not have the academic background to do so. In 1871 when Sam Grant was President, he tried to be good to the tough Westerners who had once won him a war with their blood and grit. John Lincoln Clem was commissioned as a 2nd lieutenant in the Regular 24th Infantry Regiment. He was twenty years old, five feet tall and weighed 105 pounds. He went on to a career in the Quartermaster Corps, retiring with the rank of major general in 1916. The "last man" on active duty to have served in the Civil War, he died in 1937.

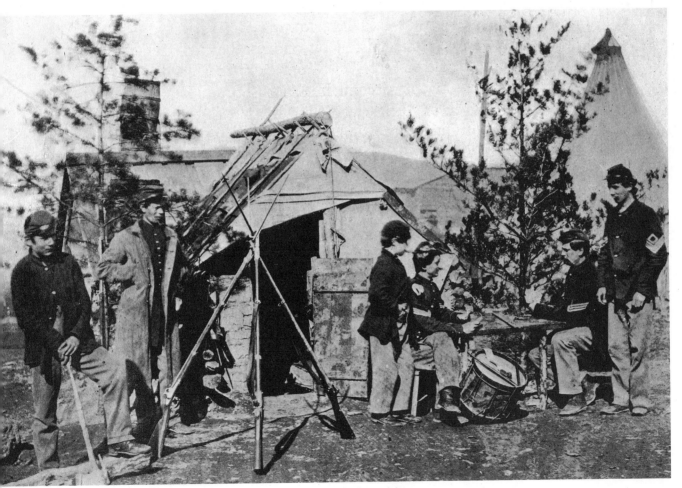

Boys leading a man's life. Drummer boys play cards with regular soldiers.

The smoky, littered battlefield belonged to the Confederates. The Rebels were tired, but glad to be alive and victorious. The soldiers of the Army of Tennessee cheered mightily and joyously when the two wings of the army joined on the slopes of the little ridge from which the Yankees had retreated. They cheered and roared on into the darkness with, as one of them said, "a tremendous swell of heroic harmony that seemed almost to lift from their roots the great trees of the forest." And the weary, grayclad soldiers tried hard not to look at the rigid dead, frozen in grotesque postures, and the torn, bloodied wounded who in so many units seemed to outnumber those left unhurt. This army that had for so long so badly needed a victory had one at last.

Yet, as ever in the Army of Tennessee, the victory was flawed. They had failed to destroy the *Army of the Cumberland*. They failed because of the lack of coordination between the two wings of the army. Had Polk's men attacked earlier in the afternoon in conjunction with Longstreet's renewed assaults, it is possible that more Union troops would have been pinned in place, unable to go to assist more vulnerable points, and consequently the Confederates might have achieved a breakthrough of Thomas' lines. But of course there can be no assurance of this.

At Chickamauga Bragg once again failed as a battlefield tactician and lost control of his army. His rigidity and indecisiveness kept him mentally chained for much too long to his original plan, which was not working. As usual, he lacked the flexibility to accept this emotionally and formulate plans better suited to the new opportunities of a fluid battle. Fearful of making decisions, he deliberately, as always, abnegated responsibility for trying to control the battle once it had begun. He failed dismally to coordinate the attacks of the two wings of his army; his troops never attacked the vulnerable gap between the two segments of Thomas' line; and at various points in the day, he either left himself utterly without reserves to exploit potential opportunities, or completely failed to see that such reserves as he did possess were brought forward into the fight at crucial times and places—as one instance, Ben Cheatham's hard-fighting men were wasted most of the afternoon. Of course the lack of initiative on the part of most of Bragg's subordinates—in contrast to the great initiative displayed by most Union officers—made it difficult for any of them to rise above the situation. And of course poorly coordinated assaults in the face of the defensive firepower of the rifle produced, as ever, fearful battle losses in the assault units. Twelve regiments of the Army of Tennessee lost more than half their men in the battle.

The numbers for both sides were grim. The Union *Army of the Cumberland* lost 6,414 men killed and missing, a significant portion of them captured, and 9,756 wounded. The Confederate Army of Tennessee lost 3,780 men killed and missing—mostly killed—and sustained 14,674 wounded, strong testimony to the efficacy of the Union improvised field defenses of breastworks. Thus, the total losses at Chickamauga were: *Army of the Cumberland*, 16,170; Army of Tennessee, 18,454. Each army lost nearly a third of its strength. One of the bloodiest battles of the war, Chickamauga was exceeded in bloodshed only by the three days of Gettysburg, and the battles of the Seven Days, both of which were waged by armies much larger in size than those of Chickamauga.

Who won the Battle of Chickamauga? The Army of Tennessee thought that it won. The *Army of the Cumberland* believed that it had lost. But they were both wrong. For Chickamauga was an indecisive bttle—another one of the numerous Civil War planned battles of destruction that did not result in the destruction of the defeated army. Civil War armies possessed too much defensive firepower and mobility to be readily destroyed. Chickamauga was merely just another Confederate tactical victory on the road to strategic defeat. Since Chickamauga was an indecisive battle, the question of who won must be deferred—it would depend upon subsequent events. And after Chickamauga, one army grew stronger and better able to fight; and the other army grew weaker and progressively more impotent. The one that grew stronger was the *Army of the Cumberland*; the side that grew weaker was the Army of the Tennessee.

Who won the Battle of Chickamauga? The Army of Tennessee thought that it won—but it lost; the *Army of the Cumberland* thought it had lost—but it won.

To understand why this was so, it is necessary to know what happened afterwards.

CHAPTER VIII

THE BLOCKADE OF CHATTANOOGA, SEPTEMBER–NOVEMBER 1863

The very indecisiveness of the Battle of Chickamauga had enormous consequences for the subsequent course of the war, for each side reacted differently in its aftermath.

Longstreet, who now had within less than three months passed through two of the goriest, most futile Southern battles of the war—Gettysburg and Chickamauga—found another indecisive, dubious victory hard to bear; the ranks of his men were being depleted in blood with little permanent good gained. So he urged Bragg to a rapid pursuit of the Yankee army on the morrow of Chickamauga, seeking his elusive battle of destruction, a decisive Confederate victory at last. But Bragg, worn and temperamentally averse to new ideas unless given time to ponder them, did not much like the sound of Longstreet's advice.

Bragg was still depressed by the failure of his own tactical plan for the battle and by what he regarded as the laxity of Bishop Polk and his men, whom he deemed primarily responsible for that failure; characteristically, he believed that he had once again been let down by disloyal subordinates. He was also sickened by the appalling casualties his army had endured; so many men that he knew personally were dead or down—a corps commander, a division commander, six brigade commanders; one brigade alone had lost half its regimental commanders. Indeed, when an officer congratulated him on a "brilliant victory," the haggard, irritable commanding general answered that his army was fearfully crippled and "horribly demoralized."

Bragg did not believe that he had won a victory, and indeed neither he nor his corps commanders were sure that the Yankees were in full retreat; everyone knew that the enemy had flinched and then pulled back—but how far back? That no one yet knew. Patrols would have to go and find out. But that would take time. A Rebel private who had been captured by the Yankees and then escaped claimed that the Federals were indeed in full flight all the way back to the Tennessee. Bragg interviewed the soldier. At one point in the talk, Bragg, dubious of the private's military knowledge, sternly asked, "Do you know what a retreat looks like?" With the casual insouciance so typical of the proud, stubborn Rebel infantryman, the soldier responded, "I ought to, General. I've been with you during your whole campaign."

Bragg considered that his smashed army did not have the impetus to take the offensive so soon. Torn units had to be reknit under new, more callow leadership; the men had to be rested and cared for. As the result of a long battle at short ranges in the woods, the loss of artillery horses had been severe, and there were now too few to haul all of the army's cannon. Nor did the army have enough food, due to the use of supply trains to haul Longstreet's infantry forward and to the breaks in the fragile rail line north of Atlanta. The Army of Tennessee had been on half-rations for three days, and the situation would get worse as the remainder of Longstreet's corps arrived in the days ahead. In any event, the army lacked the pontoons and engineering equipment needed to bridge the wild Tennessee. When advised to take the offensive, Bragg said simply but cogently, "How can I? Here is two-fifths of my army left on the field, and my artillery is without horses."

But these logical strictures were of scant concern to Longstreet, who had the memory of too many wasted dead men on his mind; Longstreet persisted in his arguments for an immediate offensive. Bragg, who already loathed Polk and Hill, did not relish Longstreet's stubbornness; the very last thing that he now needed was yet another contentious prima donna as a subordinate. Longstreet rode over to Bragg's headquarters to confront the commanding general he held in contempt.

Bragg met Longstreet on foot, and the two officers began what an observer called an "earnest conversation." Longstreet spoke quietly and calmly, but as always, very firmly. He was a man supremely sure of himself. Bragg, less secure, invariably grew excited when contradicted; his voice, too, was low, but "very angry." When Longstreet insisted that the army should be in motion, Bragg stated why this could not be done. Longstreet, never one sensitive enough to the emotions of others to know when to stop, said, "Yes, sir, but all great captains follow up a victory." That unsubtle dig was too much for Bragg, so sorely vexed by a myriad of woes both real and imagined. He reminded Longstreet of the protocol of military discipline, and appar-

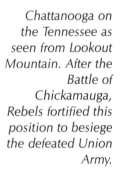

Chattanooga on the Tennessee as seen from Lookout Mountain. After the Battle of Chickamauga, Rebels fortified this position to besiege the defeated Union Army.

ently threatened him with disciplinary action for Longstreet replied grimly, "Yes, sir, you rank me, but you cannot cashier me."

It was a conflict of mind and heart. Bragg was a man of rules and numbers, seeking stern logic in an irrational world; Longstreet was a man of emotion, and so he understood much better the hearts of fighting men. Perhaps Bragg was logically correct in not wishing to subject his army to the dangers of an offensive so soon after a grueling battle. Yet, as so often, he failed to understand the emotions of those he led. His army very desperately needed a clear-cut victory to redeem itself. It needed to shed the nagging futility of its past. It needed to win for once in order to know that it could win; and so enter new battles with high, shining hopes. Bragg did not understand this, and thus, when he refused to take the offensive after Chickamauga, he smothered what embers remained of the fighting spirit of his army.

Chickamauga was not only the lost last chance for the Confederacy, it was also the lost last chance for the Army of Tennessee.

Bragg seriously did consider the possibility of an offensive in the days after Chickamauga. But, as always after a battle, he grew indecisive, unable to make up his mind lest he do the wrong thing and subject himself to the abuse that galled him so deeply from foes both imagined and real. He had ample, sound reasons not to advance so soon, and the fact that the very men he deemed most unreliable and disloyal were urging him most hotly to take the offensive doubtless helped to convince him of the impracticability of an advance. However, as Bragg thought through his tactical problem after Chickamauga, he evolved what seemed a much better plan than a reckless pursuit of the Yankee army. He would win a great victory, after all, and thus confound his critics and silence them at last; and best of all for this army whose leadership and morale he so deeply mistrusted, it

would be a victory as easy and bloodless as it was decisive. Bragg craftily intended to both eat his cake and still have it, too. For Braxton Bragg fully intended and expected to capture Chattanooga without having to fight a hard battle.

Bragg intended to move his army up to secure the dominating high ground overlooking Chattanooga and the sinuous Tennessee River. His army would be able thus to dominate the few, rough lines of supply of the Union army into the city. Some meager supplies might get through to the Federal troops over very bad, steep back roads, but not nearly sufficient to sustain the army. The Federal army would be forced to retreat before it grew too weak to either run or fight, forced to abandon Chattanooga and perhaps also disgorge most of its gains of the past nine months in Tennessee. Or, perhaps even better, although more unlikely, the Union army

The City of Chattanooga. Union troops fortified the old Confederate positions around the town as they buckled down for a long siege.

might attempt to take the offensive in order to try to gain room to open up their supply lines— and assault Bragg's army holding one of the strongest defensive positions in all of North America, a surely destructive course. Fighting defensively in such strong positions, Bragg's army would take few losses, and its deficiency in leadership and command and control would count for little in static, positional warfare; the *Army of the Cumberland* would be readily smashed, and all of Tennessee would be open to the advance of the Confederate army. It was a grand, exhilerating concept to a commander re-known but for fruitless retreats and lost victories.

Braxton Bragg planned to capture Chattanooga without having to fight hard. Bragg's plan, like many of his concepts, was logical and sound; but again like all of his designs, it took too little account of human emotion. And thus it would crumble into nothing in its execution. Bragg's grand plan would fail, not because it was a bad plan—indeed, it was a good plan—but because the Union army in Tennessee would very soon grow much stronger and more aggressive; and because his own army, which bore a now unbearable burden of failure and despondency, lacked the poise and the fighting heart to make it work.

The *Army of the Cumberland*, in apparent defeat, would grow strong and confident. The Army of Tennessee, in apparent victory, would grow weak and uncertain. After Chickamauga, Braxton Bragg's Army of Tennessee would disintegrate. But that was a failure of execution, for initially, Bragg's plan seemed to be working.

After Chickamauga, Rosecrans had retired on Chattanooga. Bragg closed in. Locked up in Chattanooga, the *Army of the Cumberland* seemed done. The troops slowly starved, their allocation of food cut to half-rations, then quarter-rations; gaunt and hollow-eyed, they grew lethargic. They survived on a few grains of parched corn and stale, rocklike hardtack. The animals died in droves—over 10,000 horses and mules—of starvation. The thin, desperate surviving horses tried to gnaw each other's tails and eat wooden hitching posts and the sides of wagons. Without animals, the army would be utterly immobilized. The *Army of the Cumberland* was too weak to fight, and soon it would be too weak to run.

Besieged troops of the Army of the Cumberland desperately wait for relief. As food and fuel ran short, there were fears that the entire army might be forced to surrender.

A cold, relentless rain fell steadily on the haggard men and suffering animals. And the enemy held the high ground all around them. A Kansas infantryman wrote of those bitter weeks in Chattanooga this way:

"So to the horrors of bitter cold and scanty clothing, of hard work and almost constant showers, of danger and ever-anxious watchfulness, was added the startling terror of want and the near approach of grim and gaunt starvation. Cattle, almost dead from lack of food, were killed and their flesh doled out in stinted quantities; the hungry and tired men haunted the slaughterhouses . . . and snatched eagerly for the hoofs, tails, heads, and entrails . . . cooking and eating with avidity garbage they would before have shrunk from in disgust . . . one day . . . a commissary train . . . arrived . . . and was unloading . . . surrounded by several hundred half-famished soldiers, who eagerly snatched and struggled for the crumbs of crackers that fell into the road from broken boxes. . . . Behind our camp was a park of artillery horses, and over them a guard had to be stationed to keep the half-starved men from taking the . . . corn doled out to the almost famished animals. The writer has seen soldiers . . . picking up the few grains of corn that had been spilled by the horses from their troughs and trampled into mud and filth underfoot. One of the regiments . . . killed and ate a dog which wandered into camp."

Lookout Mountain above the Tennessee River. Some Rebels already began to view the Federals in Chattanooga as their captives.

CROSSING THE TENNESSEE

Above: *Federal troops lay a pontoon bridge. (Brown Collection)*

Right: *"Rosey" Rosecrans romantically depicted on a songsheet leading his troops into battle. (Library of Congress)*

Below: *Federals of the Army of the Cumberland cross the Tennessee River over a pontoon bridge. Rosecrans bloodlessly outflanked Bragg, forcing him out of Chattanooga and Tennessee. (Travis Collection)*

Right: *Rosecrans at the head of a Union column under attack by Confederate forces at Murfreesboro. The Federals were only able to claim victory when Bragg retreated from the field of battle. (Kurze & Allison)*

BATTLE OF STONES RIVER

Below: *Ranks of Union and Confederate forces in combat at Murfreesboro, or Stones River. The battle was hard-fought and bloody with thousands of casualties on both sides. (Kurz & Allison)*

Braxton Bragg.

William S. Rosecrans.

BATTLE OF CHICKAMAUGA

Below, right: *Yankees and Confederates in close combat in the tangled woodlands near Chickamauga Creek. (Travis Collection)* Below: *The Union position on Snodgrass Hill on the second day of the battle of Chickamauga. The "Rock of Chickamauga," George Henry Thomas, withstood the attacks of an overwhelming number of Rebels led by one of the Confederacy's most able generals, James Longstreet. (U.S. Army Center of Military History)*

Above: General John B. Hood receives a wound to the leg while surveying the Confederate battle line at Chickamauga. His injured limb was later amputated. Hood had previously suffered the crippling loss of his left arm at Gettysburg. Below: A somewhat unrealistic portrayal of the battle of Chickamauga which raged for two days in mid-September 1863. Chickamauga was one of the bloodiest battles of the entire Civil War. (Kurz & Allison)

LOOKOUT MOUNTAIN

Left: *Hooker's divisions charge the entrenched Rebels on Lookout Mountain. Despite the generous defensive terrain, the superior Yankee numbers easily swept the Southerners out of their positions. (Kurz & Allison)*

MISSIONARY RIDGE

Below: *The Army of the Cumberland victoriously storms Missionary Ridge. Though the Federals were ordered to take the rifle pits at the base of the ridge, they surged up the hill to break the Confederate line, surprising both Union and Rebel commanders. (Kurz & Allison)*

As Thomas grimly said, "If a retreat had occured . . . it is not probable that any of the army would have reached the railroad as an organized body, if followed by the enemy." Old Rosy seemed gloomy and remote, most unlike his former self. He told Halleck, "Our loss is heavy and our troops worn down. . . . We have no certainty of holding . . . here."

The President was at first despondent at the news of Chickamauga, his brave hopes for a mortal strike into the vitals of the Confederacy dashed. But with that patient resilience so characteristic of his personality, he soon regained his elan, determined to persevere anew. As one historian perceptively noted: "The important thing . . . was not that Rosecrans had been whipped at Chickamauga, but that he still held Chattanooga."

Secretary of War Stanton, grim and zealous, intervened strongly to repair the grave damage in Tennessee. He persuaded the President to transfer two corps from Meade's *Army of the Potomac*—saying with brutally clear logic, "There is no reason to expect General Meade will attack Lee, although greatly superior in force, and his great numbers where they are are useless."—by railroad to Chattanooga. He then personally energized the railroads and the army to do the job.

This was the great railroad concentration of the campaign in Tennessee, not the more famous one of Longstreet's corps. But it is less well known because it took place after the battle along Chickamauga Creek. In less than a dozen days, 25,000 Union troops—four infantry divisions and ten batteries of artillery with all weapons and equipment and 3,000 animals—were transferred nearly 1,200 miles, the fastest overland mass movement of combat troops yet in the history of warfare.

Thus, through use of a superior railroad system, the Union was able to counter the Confederacy's assumed advantage of interior lines.

The disaster at Chickamauga cost Rosecrans his command. U.S. Grant, appointed to head military operations in the West, replaced old Rosey with George H. Thomas. Here, shiftless Yankees lounge before "Pap's" headquarters waiting for news about expected reinforcements.

THE "OTHER" RAIL REINFORCEMENT OF THE CHICKAMAUGA CAMPAIGN

Everyone is familiar with the famed railroad reinforcement of the Chickamauga Campaign. This, of course, was the decision of the Confederate leadership to detach Longstreet's corps from the Army of Northern Virginia and, utilizing the South's advantage of interior lines, send it by rail to the West in order to form a concentration with Bragg's Army of Tennessee, and thus gain a telling superiority over Rosecrans' Union *Army of the Cumberland*. It was hoped that Bragg would use his numerical advantage, so rare for a Confederate commander—indeed, one must wonder what tactical magic and enormous victory Lee would have wrought had he ever enjoyed such favorable battle odds—to crush the Union army's thrust into the Confederate heartland. The plan almost worked. But the South's limited, worn, and ramshackle railroad system could not fully support so large and rapid a deployment, with the result that only five of Longstreet's eight infantry brigades— and none of his artillery—reached Bragg in time for the Battle of Chickamauga. The Southern concentration was incomplete. This, in conjunction with Bragg's tactical clumsiness and total loss of command and control of his army, and the increased defensive firepower and infantry mobility of the rifle armies of the Civil War, doomed the Confederacy's last chance to achieve its vital but elusive battle of destruction. Chickamauga became just another Confederate tactical victory that carried the Rebels ever farther and faster down the road of strategic defeat. For the decisive railroad movement of the Chickamauga Campaign was not this famous one on the eve of the Battle of Chickamauga; it was the "other" rail movement, the Union army's, and it occurred after the battle—but not yet the campaign—had been lost.

The position of Rosecrans' army after the Battle of Chickamauga was parlous in the extreme. The *Army of the Cumberland* was stranded in Chattanooga, out on a limb at the end of a rugged, impossibly tenuous supply line, with a slightly larger, victorious Rebel army holding the dominating high ground overlooking its refuge. Each day, as men and animals consumed diminishing stocks of food, the army grew weaker. It was not strong enough to fight, and soon it would be too weak to run. Pap Thomas feared its disintegration if it were forced to retreat. The army's morale seemed low after its defeat, and its leadership seemed uncertain. Lincoln complained that Rosecrans appeared to be "confused and stunned, like a duck hit on the head." The position of the *Army of the Cumberland* seemed desperate. It needed big help in a hurry.

As so often in war, the reality was not as grim as the appearance. The young Union soldiers were resilient; they were down, but certainly not out of the fight. Pap Thomas' boys would soon show that their nation had produced no finer troops—indeed, they had already shown this, but neither they nor anyone else yet realized it, because their bitter, gallant fight along Chickamauga Creek had been part of a lost battle. Even Rosecrans, supposedly dazed by defeat and intimidated by the Rebs, had no intention of retreating, and indeed was making cogent plans to re-open his supply line; his plans were so good that they were adopted and implemented by his successor, the pragmatist Sam Grant. And best of all, the seemingly formidable Rebels were in a state of complete paralysis, unable to take any positive action, as a result of the total breakdown of command and control in Bragg's Army of Tennessee.

But in Washington the better reality was not known; only the grim possibilities of the plight of the Army of the Cumberland were fully realized. And Union leaders, led by determined Secretary of War Stanton, moved promptly and resolutely to save it.

Stanton detested most of his Union generals, whom he believed possessed insufficient ardor for the great crusade against slavery; and like many administrators he disliked the chronic negativism of technical experts, always so full of reasons why something could not be done, but barren of advice about how to get things done. In the crisis before him, Stanton wanted to switch troops by rail from George Meade's *Army of the Potomac* to the succor of Rosecrans. But Lincoln and Henry Halleck—the nearest semblance of a chief-of-staff that the army possessed in those days—objected; they said that this would prevent Meade from taking the offensive. The caustic Stanton,

Troop train loaded with men from the XI and XII Corps of the Army of the Potomac heads for Chattanooga to relieve the starved Army of the Cumberland.

who thought only slightly better of the cautious Meade than he did of the methodical Rosecrans, had the perfect response: "There is no reason to expect General Meade will attack Lee, although greatly superior in force, and his great numbers where they are are useless. In five days 30,000 could be put with Rosecrans." The President doubted Stanton's numbers; he said that he did not believe that so many troops could even be brought from Virginia to Washington, never mind distant Tennessee, in such a short time. But he did not doubt the logic of Stanton's argument. Stanton's meeting with the President ended at 0200 on 24 September. In a half-hour the energetic secretary had a telegraph message off to Meade, ordering him to detach two corps and have them fully ready to board northbound trains before nightfall that same day. He also summoned railroad officials to his office for a noon conference to work out the logistical details of the transfer.

The two corps selected to go West were Henry W. Slocum's hard-fighting *XII* and Oliver O. Howard's poorly-led and unlucky *XI*. Joe Hooker was given command of the improvised army. Hooker was able and aggressive when placed under a capable commander who could make the big and difficult decisions for him; he functioned best when he did not carry the burden of full and sole responsibility. At Chancellorsville, he had had the whole ball of wax placed in his hands, and the responsibility of being the man who could lose the Civil War in a day was too much for him; it daunted him, and he fell apart. In the West, he would have Grant's solid shoulder to lean on.

Stanton was right, and Lincoln was rarely happier to be wrong. By the evening of 30 September, the first of the Bluecoat infantrymen and artillerymen reached the Tennessee River, little more than six days from Stanton's pre-dawn meeting with Lincoln.

The infantrymen went with all of their equipment and 40 rounds per man. The gunners took along guns and caissons, horses, 200 rounds per piece, and five days' forage for the horses. In under twelve days, 25,000 Union soldiers, fully four rifle divisions and ten batteries of artillery with all of their weapons and equipment, including 3,000 horses and mules, and 100 freight cars toting baggage, were transported 1,157 miles, the swiftest mass movement of troops yet in the history of warfare: the Rebels, strong as were their efforts, had needed 17 days to send half as many men and guns 965 miles to Bragg.

It was necessary for the Union soldiers and all of their arms, supplies, equipment, baggage, and animals to change trains four times en route: the first time at Washington, where no tracks connected the two lines that had to be used; then at an unbridged crossing of the Ohio River, near Wheeling; again at Indianapolis, where no connecting link existed; and finally, at Louisville, where again no railroad bridge spanned the Ohio.

But the Yankee soldiers enjoyed their long trip toward battle. They were well provided with army rations, but better fare awaited en route, supplied by enthusiastic, patriotic people along the tracks. As a

Wisconsin infantryman gladly recalled, "Our mouths were crammed with cakes, pies, cookies, meat, eggs, and fruit, which the loyal Ohio people brought us without money or price."

Indeed, some of the soldiers enjoyed the trip a little too much. They managed to locate liquor stores near the tracks when the trains halted briefly; and some became roaring drunk, which was more than understandable in psychological terms. The trip was a transition for the men, a sharp break from their usual duties and dull army routine, a kind of a lark, and a temporary reprieve from the imminence of death, which yet they knew still awaited them somewhere up ahead at the end of the tracks in the mellow autumn days along the Tennessee River. So some of them drank too much. And a few of these fell off their box cars and sustained bad injuries; and worse, the trains had to be stopped in their relentless rush to succor Rosecrans and his beleagured men in order to pick them up. Unhappy at the delays, and always avid in the cause of sobriety, General Howard took prompt action, as he later recorded: "For some reason the Soldier's thirst for whiskey . . . seemed to be increased by the un- usual excitement of the move, and it was ordered that all liquor shops should be closed during the passage of the troops." So, sadder and drier, the Union soldiers continued westward on iron rails toward a new destiny.

There were few snags in this well organized, epic logistical feat, nothing more serious than an occasional minor delay. Yet there was one flaw in this otherwise excellent operation. The equipment placed on the trains was loaded in no particular order; hence, everything was mixed together, without regard for which items would be needed first upon disembarkation, and so that there was no logical way of finding any individual item. In World War II, the concept of "combat loading" was applied to the process of loading ships—or trains—in inverse order of need on the battlefield, so that the most vital equipment would be the most accessible and the first unloaded. Surprisingly, the American Army has had to re-learn this elementary logistical lesson anew at the outset of every subsequent war since the Civil War.

Thus, the Union was able to counter the Confederacy's advantage of interior lines through a superior railroad system. In the end, it was the Union forces that attained the telling concentration on the Tennessee at Chattanooga that the Confederate leadership had so desperately striven for. As one historian felicitously put it: ". . . for though the Confederates had stolen a march . . . the Federals had promptly upped the ante by moving farther and faster with still more."

And everyone understood who deserved most of the credit. After putting his four divisions in line below Chattanooga, Joe Hooker sent a telegraph message to Secretary Stanton. In the way of telegrams, the message was terse— and true. It read: "You may justly claim the merit of having saved Chattanooga."

Confederate partisans attempt to blow up a Federal supply train.

The Confederate leadership had desperately striven to accomplish a decisive concentration of forces in Tennessee; and they had nearly succeeded. So in the end it was the Union army that attained the decisive concentration. And thus in the end it was the Union army that won in Tennessee.

So things soon began to look much better in Chattanooga. Now Old Rosy had ample time to think; and whenever he had sufficient time to formulate his plans, he was a most formidable strategist. He went about the task of devising a plan to break the hard Rebel grip upon his supply lines. And, as usual, he came up with an excellent plan. For in their great travail that fall in Chattanooga, Old Rosy and his hard-pressed *Army of the Cumberland* were helped perhaps most of all by the lassitude and confusion of their foes.

The Army of Tennessee was slowly dying of self-inflicted wounds. Bragg's army was paralyzed in grim, futile recrimination. Its command, absorbed once again in internecine conflict, lacked the time and temper to make effective plans of war. The Confederates failed to extend their lines beyond Lookout Mountain in order to cut Chattanooga fully off from the south and west; nor did they make any attempt to cross the river and cut the city off from the north and west. The Army of Tennessee was listless; so long headless, it now increasingly was without heart, too.

Simon Bolivar Buckner. Bragg was able to purge his command of most of the generals he believed had hampered his success. In the process Buckner's command was "reshuffled."

Bragg proferred charges of disobedience of orders and neglect of duty against Bishop Polk and Tom Hindman. Polk, Longstreet, Hill, and Buckner sought to use their influence in the army and the government to have Bragg removed from command. Longstreet wrote bitterly to the Confederate War Department: "Our chief has done but one thing that he ought to have done since I joined the army. That was to order the attack upon the 20th. All other things that he has done he ought not to have done. I am convinced that nothing but the hand of God can save us or help as long as we have our present commander. . . ." In Richmond, a Confederate official noted, "Bragg and his generals quarrel. I think a general worthless whose subalterns quarrel with him. There is something wrong about the man." An officer of the Army of Tennessee said, "The tone of the army among its higher officers toward the commander was the worst conceivable. Bragg was the subject of hatred and contempt, and it was almost openly so expressed."

President Davis himself came personally to Tennessee to undertake the hopeless task of resolving the mortal conflicts in the command structure of the Army of Tennessee. He was confronted by officers who openly stated that they had no confidence in the leadership of their commanding general, an impossible situation. But Davis stubbornly would not replace Bragg. He kept Bragg in command because he did not believe that there was a suitable replacement in view. He hated Joe Johnston, and that officer had not displayed much of his alleged talent in his Western commands, and had already nettled the President by refusing the government's earlier pleas to take over in Tennessee. Longstreet may well still have wanted the job, but Davis did not esteem his abilities, and Longstreet did not help his chances by playing hard to get, expressing the thought that the army's one great opportunity for victory had already been squandered. So in the end Davis sustained Bragg, an horrendous error. The President held up Harvey Hill's commission as lieutenant general. Bishop Polk clearly could not serve longer with Bragg, and was transferred elsewhere. Bragg then augmented the bitterness by relieving Hill; cranky, unloved, and comparatively new to the army, Hill had the shallowest roots in it, and was easiest to weed out. Buckner and Walker were too well liked in the army, and Longstreet had too much prestige, to be made scapegoats for the failure to achieve decisive victory under Bragg's revered plan at Chickamauga. So Hill became the scapegoat, to the joy of the many who knew and disliked him, and to the satisfaction of Bragg. And then Bragg, who was also a man who did not know— or, by now, care—when to relent, reshuffled the organization of his units so as to render impotent Buckner and the hostile Tennessee-Kentucky factions in the army; Ben Cheatham requested that he be relieved of duty in Bragg's command. Only Walker and Longstreet now remained in positions of significance. And Bragg and Longstreet barely spoke to each other. Indeed, Bragg was planning to rid himself of this Virginia prima donna soon, too.

As an historian of the Army of Tennessee explained, "Relations between Longstreet and Bragg deteriorated so badly that the Virginia general maintained an almost isolated command on Lookout Mountain. The two held no discussion as to how the Federals should be kept bottled up. . . . Longstreet seemed totally disinterested in affairs west of the mountain." So because of the lethargy bred by command chaos, the leaders of the Army of Tennessee failed to exploit their most commanding position and extend their lines so as to fully cut off Chattanooga from the south and west, much less the north. And shrewd Old Rosy was precisely the officer to devise a plan to take advantage of so large a deficiency. But the carrying out of the plan would devolve upon others. For the *Army of the Cumberland,* too, was to be much altered by changes in command.

Exactly one month after the first day of Chickamauga, Rosecrans was relieved of command of the *Army of the Cumberland,* a victim of Stanton's wrath and his own mournful messages, which persuaded Lincoln that his resolve had left him. The unfortunate McCook, his corps always routed, and Crittenden, who had had little role at Chickamauga, as most of his command had been dispersed and sent to the support of Thomas, were fired first, perhaps on the reasonable theory that luckless generals were almost as dangerous as bad generals, but more realistically as scapegoats for the army's flight; and, as Stanton then acidly observed, if they had "made pretty good time away from the fight . . . Rosecrans beat them both." Inevitably, Pap Thomas was given the job, and this time he was pleased to accept it. Thomas' men were joined by Maj. Gen. Joseph Hooker's command, a pair of corps from the *Army of the Potomac.* And another new force would soon arrive from the West, the *Army of the Tennessee,* commanded by bright, bandy-legged Maj. Gen. William

After Chickamauga, U.S. Grant, hero of Fort Donnelson, Shiloh and Vicksburg, took command of the Western Theatre. Grant's success at Chattanooga won him the position of General-in-Chief of the entire Union armed forces.

Tecumseh Sherman. Above all, a new man arrived to take command of these varied forces, indeed to take command of all Union troops in the vast area between the Allegheny Mountains and the Mississippi River—a rumpled, sandy-haired man named Grant, Maj. Gen. Hiram Ulysses "Sam" Grant.

Sam Grant was a laconic Western pragmatist; he was not interested in abstractions—only in results. Not an intellectual soldier, but a flexible one, he had no pet theories to shelter from the hard test of combat reality, and he called no single style of warfare his own. In his campaigns in the West, his operations with the Navy on the rivers showed a matchless grasp of amphibious warfare; his Mississippi campaign was a masterpiece of stunning mobility, an early day blitzkrieg; and in the East he would rely on massive frontal concentrations to immobilize and enervate a faster, but weaker, foe. Concerned only with results, he was hard on subordinate commanders; yet he also tended to make pets of officers he deemed had served him well in the past, for loyalty was one of his largest virtues. Billy Sherman, for instance, could do no wrong.

Rosecrans had failed, so Grant was not reluctant to order his removal. The dapper, thoughtful Rosecrans did not much like the slouched, terse, down-to-earth Grant, and was much disappointed by his relief from command, but he did not sulk, hoping for the failure of his successor; he was a patriot and a gentleman. So

William Farrar "Baldy" Smith organized the "Cracker-Line" relief effort to supply the besieged Army of the Cumberland at Chattanooga.

graciously he sought out Grant and told him of his plan to relieve the desperate supply situation of the army in Tennessee. As Grant said, " . . . he described very clearly the situation at Chattanooga, and made some excellent suggestions as to what should be done." And then, with a simple, mordant truth, Grant epitomized Rosecrans as a commander—the man of ample thought, but less ample action—by adding, "My only wonder was that he had not carried them out."

It turned out to be an easy thing. The idea came out of the fertile but contentious brain of Rosecrans' chief engineer officer, Brig. Gen. W. F. "Baldy" Smith. A portly, argumentative officer, Smith's career advancement had been hindered by his acerbic personality; he had departed the Eastern army unpromoted due to conflicts with his superiors. It says much for Rosecrans' intelligence that he was able to nurture and thus get such good use out of so touchy a man. And when Grant arrived, no time was lost putting the Smith-Rosecrans plan into effect. Enough time had been lost already, for it was late October. Sam Grant was also a mover.

Union troops drill in preparation for a rematch with the Rebs who had defeated them at Chickamauga.

CHAPTER IX

CHATTANOOGA RELIEVED, 25 OCTOBER–23 NOVEMBER 1863

Joe Hooker's men set out first, marching west on 25 October. They crossed the Tennessee River down at Bridgeport on the night of the 26th, and three divisions—about 11,000 troops—marched north into the region west of Lookout Mountain, left utterly undefended by the comatose, quarrelsome Confederates. Meanwhile, a combat team of two infantry brigades and an engineer battalion—about 3,500 troops—led by Baldy Smith crossed on a pontoon bridge north of Chattanooga and moved quietly westward toward Brown's Ferry, on the north side of the Tennessee; when they reached their objective, they took cover in the brush and waited. And at 0300 on 27 October a picked group of 1,500 soldiers from Thomas' units were loaded aboard sixty floating pontoons at the Chattanooga docks. The lines were cast off, and the improvised barges floated downstream on the powerful current in a hazy mist. One soldier fell overboard, but had to be left, screaming, in the water to drown; the boats had to reach their destination before dawn. And they did.

At 0500 Thomas' men jumped ashore on the south side of the river, out of the morning mist, and captured the few Rebel pickets holding the west bank opposite Brown's Ferry. The boats then crossed the river to pick up Smith's men and ferry them across. Then, while the infantrymen protected them, the combat engineers anchored the pontoons in the river and decked them over. The Union army was putting a bridge across the Tennessee River, one out of the range of most of the Confederate guns on the high ground east of Chattanooga. Baldy Smith's excellent scheme had utilized innovative military concepts such as combined arms combat teams and a commando raid to achieve remarkable success at little cost. Baldy Smith was right. It was an easy thing.

Then some of the infantry units marched southwest to join up with the more formidable hosts of Joe Hooker. The rest remained behind to protect the bridge. Soon after dawn, the Rebels awoke to the surprise in their midst. They had but a single brigade—E. McIvor Law's Alabamans—dispersed at various sites west of Lookout Mountain. Elements of this brigade attacked the more numerous Union infantry holding in a strong defensive perimeter west of the bridge; the Rebel assault was readily broken up by intense fire, and the grayclad infantry forced to retreat without accomplishing anything. They were too few, too late.

Meanwhile, the units under Hooker's command struck hard directly west clearing Cummings Gap through Raccoon Mountain, driving off the light Confederate infantry screens along the road, and assaulting up the mountain in order to overrun and capture the Rebel artillery emplaced there. Then the Union troops drove straight to the Tennessee again at Kelley's Ferry. The Union army now had a direct line of supply from the west—north—bank of the Tennessee at Kelley's Ferry, through Cummings Gap, to Brown's Ferry, and then to the bridge north of Chattanooga and on into the city itself. It was a line which could be defended with much more ample numbers than the Confederates might deploy against it, as long as the Union forces controlled the bridge at Brown's Ferry. Because of the prominence of hardtack and crackers in their daily ration, the troops called the new supply route, the "Cracker Line." The Confederate siege of Chattanooga—such as it was—was thus readily broken. It was an easy thing.

The Confederate command system was unable to respond promptly to so rapid and decisive a challenge. Longstreet, showing why Davis had refused to entrust him with com-

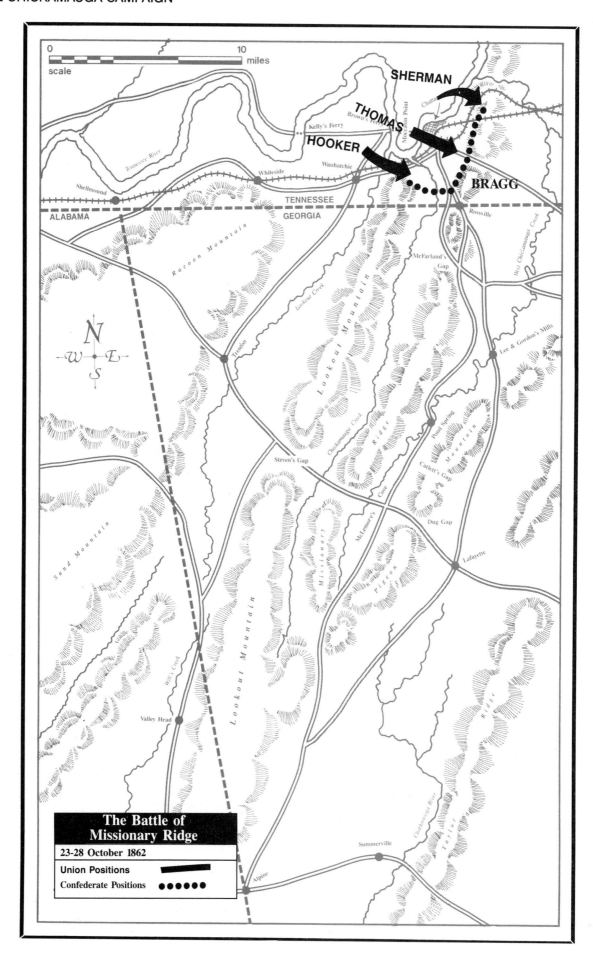

The Battle of
Missionary Ridge

23-28 October 1862

Union Positions

Confederate Positions

Joseph Hooker (1814–1879)

A native of Massachusetts, Hooker was educated in local schools and graduated from West Point 29th in the class of 1837. He served with great distinction in the Mexican War, winning three brevets, and subsequently on the Pacific Coast. He resigned from the army in 1853 after a two year leave of absence, and unsuccessfully took up farming in northern California and entered the militia. He endeavored to reenter the army in 1858 but his application was ignored and his fortunes steadily declined. He returned to the army on the outbreak of the Civil War, being made a brigadier general of volunteers in August of 1861. He commanded a brigade in the defenses of Washington, and a division in the *Army of the Potomac* in the Peninsular Campaign, serving in *III Corps,* during which he earned his nickname, "Fighting Joe Hooker," as a result of a telegraphic error in a newspaper story. In the peninsula, during the Second Bull Run Campaign, and at Antietam, Hooker displayed considerable talents as a soldier, rising to the command of *I Corps.* At Fredericksburg he was given overall direction of several corps comprising the Federal center. His severe criticism of Maj. Gen. Ambrose E. Burnside's conduct of this battle precipitated the latter's relief. Hooker, who was politically connected with Secretary of the Treasury Salmon P. Chase and several other cabinet members was named to replace Burnside. He proved an able and popular administrator, but a terrible supreme commander, developing a brilliant plan for the Chancellorsville Campaign but totally botching its execution. His confusion during the early days of the Gettysburg Campaign led to his removal on 28 June. Subsequently he commanded the pair of corps sent West in September, serving with some distinction in the operations around Chattanooga. Nevertheless, he was relieved "at his own request" late in 1863 and saw no further combat service, retiring from the Regular Army as a major general in 1868. Hooker was an excellent example of an officer promoted beyond his abilities. A quite good corps commander, he was inept and confused when given an army.

mand of the army, languidly insisted that the attack at Brown's Ferry was merely a diversion to draw Confederate strength from the advantageous positions on the high ground. So he did nothing while Hooker's troops tramped steadily to render the vital Union bridge invulnerable. Bragg was, as usual, both angry and unsure; he thought that something should be done to dislodge the Yankees from the region west of Lookout Mountain, but he did not know what.

Steamships brought supplies to the troops of Chattanooga. Most of the food that was sent to the Army of the Cumberland came in the form of bland but durable cracker-like hardtack, a major staple in the diet of the Union soldiers. For this reason, the supply line that these ships created was known as the "Cracker-Line."

Rebels fortified Lookout Mountain.

Hooker and his staff before the attack on Lookout Mountain. Taking the Rebel positions on the heights was originally believed to be a costly task. Yet, the Easterners easily pushed their adversaries out of their way. Below: Camps of the XI and XII Corps situated below the ominous Lookout Mountain. The Yankees would have to make their assault in full view of the Confederates.

Previous page: Confederate guerrillas raid a Union supply train on its way to Chattanooga.

Above: *To get to Chattanooga, supply wagons had to cross mountainous terrain and hostile territory. More often than not, these supply trains were easy targets for Confederate raiders.*

The hatred between Bragg and Longstreet made effective communication between them impossible. Longstreet, awaking but slowly to the danger as reports came in of increasing Federal strength to the west, decided—at last—on the 28th to essay an attack. But instead of using all three of the divisions in his corps, he committed only one, and instead of striking north toward the vital point, Brown's Ferry, he struck three miles south, at a division which Hooker had dropped off to protect his rear. Once again, Old Peter would be victim of his own stubbornness; he could not quite admit that he was wrong, that Brown's Ferry was most

certainly not a diversion, but instead was the keystone of the entire Union operation. So he hedged his bet, and committed but one division to the assault, and that in the wrong place.

Bragg assumed that Longstreet was assaulting Brown's Ferry with his full strength; but as usual, he neither ordered him to do so, nor checked up through members of his staff to ascertain what Longstreet was doing. Bragg lost control of the battle even before it had begun. It was an old story in his army.

Longstreet's misbegotten night attack was a fiasco. The four Confederate brigades were unable to coordinate their movements in the dark, and the battle dissolved into an indecisive long-range firefight, men on both sides shooting at red flashes in the night. Hooker hied reinforcements south, and the confused Rebel units retreated.

Over the next few days, the Confederate commanders desultorily debated the merits of an attack west of Lookout Mountain; but this was impossible. By now the Yankees were much too strong in number, held commanding ground, and Thomas could reinforce Hooker at will thanks to the bridge at Brown's Ferry. It was too late—much too late.

Unable to deal with the grim reality of their strategic dilemma, Bragg and Longstreet sought to focus on a fantasy. Encouraged by Davis, both men deemed it a good idea to detach two divisions under Longstreet to East Tennessee to confront Burnside. This, it was hoped, would force the Union commanders to send troops from Chattanooga to help sustain Burnside. While this plan to weaken the Army of Tennessee in the face of the ever increasing power and boldness of its adversaries was strategic lunacy—the original Confederate plan of concentration in Tennessee was now giving way to a new scheme of dispersal in Tennessee—Bragg eagerly but foolishly grasped this chance to rid himself of the last of his unreliable prima donna subordinates. He was happy to be done with the stubborn Georgian—who was glad to be gone—although the misguided transfer would reduce his strength to about 43,000 troops in seven divisions, while Grant's army grew to about 75,000 troops in thirteen divisions.

The problems of Grant's army at the time were of lesser importance, though nevertheless real. One problem was the new commanding general himself. Fiercely loyal to proven friends, Grant was cold to soldiers he deemed deficient or unproven. And he was not favorably impressed by George H. Thomas. He mistakenly read in Thomas' methodical ways and care for the lives of his men an unseemly prudence. Thomas was too slow and cautious, he believed. Even more remarkably, he persuaded himself that Thomas' men lacked grit and would not fight hard! Indeed, he confided to his pet, wily Billy Sherman—who in fact had much in common as a tactician with Thomas, a fact that Grant would never permit himself to see—that he believed Thomas' troops "had been so demoralized by the Battle of Chickamauga that he feared they could not be got out of their trenches to assume the offensive." So Thomas was timid, and his men only suited for static roles in positional warfare. And Grant, full of himself after his great triumph at Vicksburg, did not take much care to conceal this opinion. Sherman knew it, and Sherman's men sensed it; they learned to mistrust and doubt the Cumberlanders, who in turn raged inwardly at the quiet but real disdain of their fellow Westerners.

Another difficulty was the conflict between Hooker's men and the Western soldiers. The rangy, crude, individualistic Western troops had little regard for the men from the *Army of the Potomac*, an opinion apparently not shared by Grant. They jeered them as effete, rigid, "paper-collar" soldiers and shouted "Bull Run!" and "All quiet on the Potomac!" at them; and they told each other, "What elegant corpses they'll make in those fine clothes!" The Eastern men looked askance at the insouciance, informality, crudity, and ignorance of the Western soldiers; as one said disdainfully, "Except for the color of their uniforms, they looked exactly like the rebels." But these were minor problems compared with those of Bragg's army. The limited—but brilliant—operations of late October had gained for the Union forces in the Chattanooga area a secure line of supply and some room to maneuver. As the army renewed its strength, Grant contemplated taking the offensive.

CHAPTER X

MISSIONARY RIDGE, 25 NOVEMBER 1863

Grant's plan to drive the Confederates from the high ground around Chattanooga partly reflected his understanding of the various mutual misconceptions and divisive emotions in his army. The main role in the battle was to go to Sherman's men, the *Army of the Tennessee,* who arrived on 15 November. They were to attack the northern spur of Missionary Ridge, take it, and then climb to the main ridgeline and drive south across it to take the strong Rebel positions in flank. Hooker's Easterners also had a major role. His troops were to essay a pinning attack on the other flank, and make such progress as they could. But Thomas' sulky Cumberlanders were handed a demeaning task. To begin with, Thomas was stripped of two divisions, one-third of his command, sent to support the main attacks. Then his units were ordered to advance straight up the valley against the center of the Confederate line as a diversion.

Missionary Ridge was a steep series of hills running roughly north-south, linked by deep, broken gullies and strewn with brush, rocks, and fallen trees. At 1530 on the afternoon of 25 November, after a day of listening to the din of battle in the sky on both flanks, Thomas' men stepped out across the valley to assault the Confederate trench at the base of the ridgeline. Baird's division advanced on Thomas' left, then came Wood's division, and then Sheridan's, and on the right, Johnson's: they totaled sixty regiments, about 25,000 grim infantrymen with much to prove. There was about a mile of open ground to the bottom of the ridge, and soon the rebel artillery began to fire. Black blossoms rose amid the relentlessly advancing infantry, but the fire was neither intense nor accurate, for due to the steepness of the ridge, the Confederate gunners had difficulty in depressing their guns sufficiently to hit much in the valley below. But the fire was heavy enough for Thomas' lead

units to break into a run, trying to cover that stretch of open ground as rapidly as possible, trying to spend little time in the zone slashed by fire, running hard to make up for the bitter defeat at Chickamauga that they did not know was not a defeat. And as they ran, they yelled to each other to remember: "Chickamauga! Chickamauga!" Thomas' men screamed as they charged.

The numbers and determination of the charging Cumberlanders were too much for the Rebel riflemen to stand; they could easily see that they were destined to lose, overwhelmed and overlapped by a furious, surging, relentless tide of angry men in dark blue coats with a lost battle two months old on their minds. The Confederate troops buckled, then broke, a few trying to scamper back up the slope behind the trench, most simply flinging away their rifles and thoughtfully putting up their arms. Soon it was clear that George Thomas' men had done their job. But elsewhere the battle was not going at all as Sam Grant expected.

The Confederate line was overextended, concentrated in the center, but spread much too thin to the south. Hooker's men, after much hard fighting, prevailed, driving in the left flank of Bragg's line. But Sherman's vaunted fighters had made scant progress. Bloodily impeded by rough terrain and the fierce fire of Pat Cleburne's tough men. Billy Sherman's men were stopped.

Grant impassively brooded as to how to best recast his plans; hopefully, Hooker's men could keep advancing. And then, spontaneously, George Thomas' men did the unasked, the unexpected—the unbelievable. They began to scale the ridge.

Down in the former Confederate trench, Thomas' officers were bawling for their men to dig up dirt and pile it to cover the unprotected

Western Yankees drill near Missionary Ridge. Lookout Mountain was a sideshow compared to the task the Army of the Cumberland faced in attacking the strong Confederate positions of Missionary Ridge.

Following: *Lookout Mountain as seen from the banks of the Tennessee near Chattanooga.* Inset: *Rebel entrenchments on Lookout Mountain. Hooker's troops struggled over this rugged terrain to do battle with elements of the Army of Tennessee.*

Hooker's Easterners charge the Rebels on Lookout Mountain. Since the Federals strongly outnumbered their antagonists, they seized control of the heights with little difficulty.

Lookout Mountain the day after the battle.

rear parapet. The soldiers were milling uncertainly, restlessly. They began to take heavy, sustained rifle fire from Confederate infantrymen higher up the steep ridge. They were scared. And then they were mad. They wanted to get out from under the fierce fire from above. They wanted to attack and pay the Rebels back for Chickamauga. They wanted to show Sam Grant what hard-fighting men really looked like. And they wanted to pay a debt to good Old Pap Thomas. So, at first in little groups of friends, and then in squads, and platoons, and companies, and finally in their regiments, they climbed that steep, rough slope, advancing crouched and grim and strangely glad up into that torrent of fire from above.

At first their officers tried to stop their mad, unordered charge, then caught up by the fierce, determined spirit of the men, their officers instead began to follow the troops up the hill, yelling from habit as they advanced, "Follow me!" even as they were following their men.

Grant was appalled and astounded. Men followed orders in his command, and besides, no mortal men could storm that ridge in a frontal assault. Thomas' divisions would be bled white for no purpose. He turned angrily on Thomas, asking impatiently, "Thomas, who ordered those men up the ridge." As always, Thomas responded quietly and placidly, "I don't know. I did not." Still angry, Grant wondered if all of these unpredictable Cumberlanders were crazy! Indeed, he had just had to reprimand the redoubtable Gordon Granger—a corps commander now, and no doubt also now better loved in the army—for forgetting his duties as a general officer to help enthusiastically man and fire an artillery piece at the Rebels to support his infantrymen down below. Grant turned on Granger and asked shortly, "Did you order them up, Granger?" Granger could not conceal the glee in his hard-fighting soul at this unexpected development as he answered, "No. They started up without orders." And then he added, in a little dig at the commanding general's silly mistrust of Thomas and his men, "When those fellows get started all hell can't stop them." Grant turned away, remarking that commands would be lost if that mad charge was beaten. But George Thomas did not worry. And he was

proud of his men.

And so Thomas' men, slipping and bent over, gasping for breath, hearing the sharp, stinging buzz of enemy bullets in their ears, and sometimes the smacking, sucking noise of a round smashing into some unlucky man nearby, advanced.

At the base of the ridge, Phil Sheridan watched his men climb, hoping that they would reach the top ahead of Wood's men, off to the left; a staff officer offered him a drink of whiskey from a silver flask. Sheridan took a long pull and then started on up the hill himself.

The slow, relentless, seemingly irresistible advance of the broken lines of grim, resolute blue infantrymen spooked the Confederate defenders. They had the firepower and the cover to defeat this attack, just as Grant feared. But they became victims of a not unusual phenomenon of the modern battlefield, what that greatest of all writers of infantry combat, S. L. A. Marshall, would come to term "combat isolation." The Rebel infantrymen were concealed and dispersed amid the brush, rocks, and trees. They could not see each other; they could not take strength from the assured presence of trusted comrades. Each man felt himself alone, isolated, facing by himself the thousands of the enemy he could see spread out before him, convinced that all of those grim, implacable, furious foes were coming at him, and him alone. It was too much for them to bear. Some of the finest infantry the world would ever see, in a robust defensive position, broke and fled. And by 1630 hours George Thomas' underdogs took Missionary Ridge. The Gateway to the South had been kicked wide open.

Gordon Granger, enjoying this sweet time of redemption and revenge for this basely maligned army, rode among his infantrymen, laughing madly, and chortling sarcastically in manic parody of Grant's strictures, "I'm going to have you all court-martialed! You were ordered to take the works at the foot of the hill and you've taken those on top! You have disobeyed orders, all of you, and you know that you ought to be court-martialed!"

It was a joyous day for the Cumberlanders and Old Pap Thomas.

At left:
*Rossville Gap at Missionary Ridge on the day
after.* Below: *Lookout Mountain, where Hooker
was ordered to strike the Confederate left.*

Yankees engage Rebels at Missionary Ridge. After Sherman's assault on the Rebel right at Missionary Ridge failed, the Army of the Cumberland was sent to assault the center of the enemy line. While a disastrous situation similar to Pickett's charge could have resulted, the Federals were easily able to take the ridge.

Federals storm the heights of Missionary Ridge. Originally, the Army of the Cumberland intended to take rifle pits at the base of Missionary Ridge. However, anxious to redeem their honor after Chickamauga, the Westerners raced to the fortifications at the summit. The stunned Confederates quickly dispersed as the vengeful Yankees broke through the Rebel line.

Above: *A victorious Grant surveys the battleground of Lookout Mountain.* At right: *Officers view their commander.*

THE CHICKAMAUGA-CHATTANOOGA NATIONAL MILITARY PARK

The Chickamauga-Chattanooga National Military Park was established by act of Congress in 1890 and was dedicated five years later. In the era of increased nationalism that followed the Compromise of 1877, when Northeners and Southerners alike were eager to put behind them the tension and bitterness of long years of sectional strife and gladly sponsored a variety of symbols of national unity, the time was propitious for such an undertaking.

The park may thus be perceived as more than a memorial to the men in blue and gray who fought so hard so long ago in those dusky, smoky Tennessee woodlands; it is also a symbol of national re-unification. This symbolism is best perceived in the tall column of the New York Monument on Lookout Point, which holds statues of two soldiers—one Union and one Confederate—shaking hands.

The park is the most extensive and sprawling of the national military parks; it covers 8,500 acres. One may take a self-guided, eight-mile automobile tour of the battlefield. There are many monuments of marble, granite, and limestone, as well as batteries of field guns and round, iron cannon balls, to mark the progress of this complex fight, indicate key terrain, and laud important units. The Fuller Collection of American Military Arms, located in the park

Spoils of the victor.

More captured weapons the Rebels could ill afford to lose. After Missionary Ridge, Bragg did a great service to the Confederacy: he resigned. However, the damage had already been done.

headquarters and museum building, contains one of the best collections of shoulder arms in America, including several rare and unique rifles.

The reconstructed Brotherton cabin marks the site of the breakthrough of Longstreet's fierce, yelling men. The imposing limestone Wilder Monument rises to a height of 86 feet, and within the castle-turret-like structure a spiral staircase leads to a platform at the top that offers a good view of the battlefield; it perpetuates the memory of John Wilder's hard-fighting brigade of Union mounted infantry. The log cabin on Snodgrass Hill marks the whereabouts of the last stand of the defeated Union forces, who were saved for better days by the courage and coolness of the redoubtable Pap Thomas. At Point Park, Lookout Mountain, is the Ochs Observatory and Museum, which, high above the winding Tennessee River, offers

one of the most magnificent vistas in the South.

The best description of the park is to be found in John R. Sullivan's *Chickamauga and Chattanooga Battlefields* (Washington, 1956).

Within a few hours' driving distance is the Stones River National Military Park and Cemetery, at Murfreesboro, Tennessee, where Old Rosy Rosecrans and Braxton Bragg began the Tennessee campaign that would end almost a full year later, after some of the hardest, bloodiest fighting of the Civil War, with the legendary assault of Thomas' fired-up men along the broken, steep slopes of Missionary Ridge.

An unusual coincidence once occurred at the site of the Chickamauga battlefield. One of Tom Hindman's Mississippi infantry officers had part of his jawbone and some teeth torn away by a minie ball at Chickamauga. Then, thirty-two years later, the officer

and others of his former company were attending a reunion at the battlefield, and they passed through the area where he had been hit. One of the men caught sight of something in the dirt; he bent down and picked up three molars, calling out to the former officer, "Captain, here are your teeth." And the Mississippi captain said they were his.

And so, as one historian wrote nearly a century after the Battle: "Moonlight still glimmers on Chickamauga's creek. The dark woods through which it winds are brighter for their memories of valor. Autumn mist still veils Lookout Mountain, mist that frames a shining vision.

" 'Fierce, fiery warriors fight upon the clouds. . . .' Now it is only the elements, with rolling thunder and bolts of flashing lightning, that storm Missionary Ridge, as gallant men did . . . [in] 1863."

Missionary Ridge, where the Army of the Cumberland showed bravery and daring.

CHAPTER XI

THE GATEWAY OPENED

Although Phil Sheridan's division pressed on beyond Missionary Ridge for some distance after the crest was siezed by Thomas' elated troops, Grant was unable to organize a pursuit. That night Bragg pulled his army back, not halting until he was 50 miles inside Georgia.

For Braxton Bragg Chattanooga was the bitter end of nearly a year of defeat rendered inevitable by his own methods and personality. He shortly resigned his command of the Army of Tennessee. Yet that would not solve the deep problems of that troubled army. In December Joe Johnston took over. The armies soon went into winter quarters. And in March of 1864 Grant went East, to be replaced by Sherman. In May Sherman launched his armies on the road to Atlanta. Johnston lacked the aggressiveness to cope with Billy Sherman's mobile tactics, and his frequent strategic withdrawals hurt the morale of his army. In July Johnston was replaced by fighting, dauntless John Bell Hood, but his corps commanders thought him too callow and reckless and sought to hinder his orders and obey him only conditionally, a familiar vice of this gallant but badly led army destined to know only spoiled, lost victories and sour defeats.

In a way it was most fitting that it was their old adversaries, the Cumberlanders, who first gave the Army of Tennessee a bad, bitter defeat.

Thus, as the weary grayclad infantry moved off into the gathering darkness on 25 November, beaten and depressed, retreating from the battleground of Missionary Ridge, a thoughtful Southern lieutenant said to his company commander, "Captain, this is the death knell of the Confederacy. If we cannot cope with those fellows with the advantages we had on this line, there is not a line between here and the Atlantic Ocean where we can stop them."

The young Confederate officer was right.

It would have gladdened the hearts of Pap Thomas' men to hear.

So it was worth repeating.

All the fighting and marching, glory and bitterness of the Chickamauga Campaign bore fruit when George Thomas' underdogs—*The Army of the Cumberland*—took Missionary Ridge and kicked the Gateway to the South wide open. It was a grand, sweet, joyous day for the Cumberlanders and Old Pap Thomas.

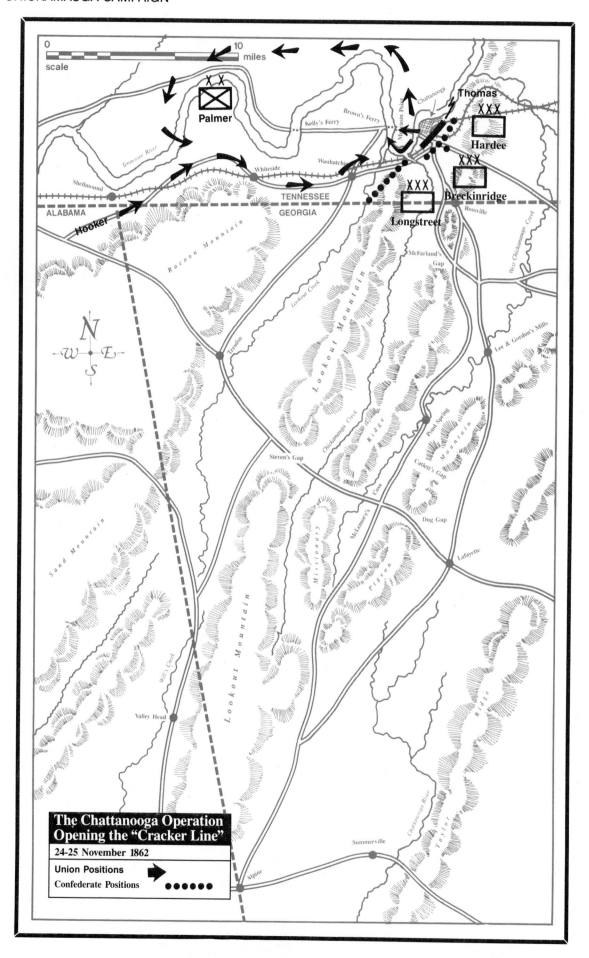

**The Chattanooga Operation
Opening the "Cracker Line"**

24-25 November 1862

Union Positions
Confederate Positions

Welcome supply boat arrives at Chattanooga.

Riverboats resupply the Federal forces after the victorious battles of Missionary Ridge and Lookout Mountain. The rugged terrain of the area made the river transport ideal.

Philip Sheridan.

At right: *William Tecumseh Sherman launched his epic march on Atlanta from Chattanooga. His campaign was based on the victories of the Chickamauga campaigns.* Below: *Missionary Ridge as seen from the Tennessee River. While the Chickamauga campaign is not as well known as the more famous Eastern battles, the exploits of the Army of the Cumberland mark a significant chapter in the Civil War, as well as U.S. history.*

Above: *Confederate prisoners at Chattanooga. After Bragg's failures during the Chickamauga campaign, the Confederacy's fate was sealed.*
At right: *Victorious XX Corps of the Army of the Cumberland parades through Washington after the war.*

GUIDE FOR THE INTERESTED READER

Recommended Reading

The literature on the Chickamauga Campaign is fairly extensive and what follows should be considered merely as a set of particularly useful or unusually interesting works.

NON-FICTION

For a general analysis of the strategy, tactics, and logistics of the Civil War nothing surpasses Herman Hattaway's and Archer Jones' *How the North Won, A Military History of the Civil War* (Urbana, Ill, 1983), which is large, brilliant, comprehensive, scholarly, and interesting all at once. This may be usefully supplemented by several other works. Grady McWhiney's and Perry D. Jamieson's *Attack and Die, Civil War Military Tactics and the Southern Heritage* (University, Ala, 1982) is an interesting and important, if flawed, work in which the authors generate some perceptive insights, but then frequently overstate their case and insert an ethnic argument which makes them the laughing stock of historians; yet they deserve credit for drawing attention to an important subject and stimulatng the work of other scholars. David Donald's essay "Refighting the Civil War," in his *Lincoln Reconsidered, Essays on the Civil War Era* (New York, 1956) is a thoughtful, seminal discussion of Civil War strategy and tactics in the age of the rifle and the railroad to which all who write on these subjects must remain indebted. The companion volumes to *The Chickamauga Campaign,* David G. Martin's *The Shiloh Campaign* (New York, 1987) and Albert A. Nofi's *The Gettysburg Campaign* (New York, 1986) are also of use for their treatment of various technical aspects of military life and practice during the Civil War.

For the overall operations encompassing the Chickamauga Campaign, Shelby Foote's *Fred-*

icksburg to Meridian, Volume II of his *The Civil War: A Narrative* (New York, 1963), is not likely to be surpassed. As befits a novelist, Foote writes exceedingly well, and he had a fine gift for description and pungent insights and judgments. As inevitable in a work on such a grand scale, there are a few minor errors, but this remains, nevertheless a distinguished work, pleasing both to the general reader and the scholar.

Fairfax Downey's *Storming the Gateway, Chattanooga, 1863* (New York, 1960) is a very readable account of the campaign. Downey writes well, with a wealth of anecdotes—including several about drummer-boy Sergeant Clem—and also has the best account of the "other" railroad concentration of the campaign. Despite some minor errors, this is an enjoyable and worthwile work.

On the Battle of Chickamauga proper, Glenn Tucker's *The Battle of Chickamauga* (Harrisburg, Pa, 1969), a brief introductory work, general but essentially sound, is a good place for a neophyte to begin, while his *Chickamauga: Bloody Battle of the West* (Indianapolis, 1961), a popular work with some scholarly credibility, is a more intensive, more serious presentation. Like all of Tucker's works, these are well written, richly anecdotal, and very interesting, though Tucker is opinionated.

The Confederate Army of Tennessee has received some attention in the literature. Thomas L. Connelly's *Autumn of Glory, The Army of Tennessee, 1862–1865* (Baton Rouge, 1971) is a reliable, dispassionate, scholarly account, the author striving with remarkable success to be just to both Bragg and his subordinates. Connelly's treatment is excellent with regard to Bragg's disruptive personality and the specifics of his clumsy tactics, as well as the progressive paralysis of command and control in Bragg's army. Stanley F. Horn's older, scholarly *The Army of Tennessee* (Indianapolis, 1941) still remains useful on the topic as well. The Union *Army of the Cumberland* is well served by Francis F. McKinney's *Education in Violence: The Life of George H. Thomas and the History of the Army of the Cumberland* (Detroit, 1961), a fine work, at once scholarly, interesting, and insightful, which deserves to be far better known.

The two other principal commanders in the Chickamauga Campaign have also received some valuable attention in the literature. William M. Lamers' *The Edge of Glory: A Biography of General William S. Rosecrans* (New York, 1961) is a useful treatment of the life of the commander of the *Army of the Cumberland.* Grady McWhiney's *Braxton Bragg and the Confederate Defeat* (New York, 1969) is a useful work in which the author renders some strong judgments.

FICTION
There are no fictional treatments of interest in which the Chickamauga Campaign figures.

JOURNALS
The principal journals treating of the Civil War are *Civil War Times Illustrated, Blue and Gray,* and *Civil War History. The Civil War Book Exchange* is a valuable guide to the current literature. Several military journals regularly publish Civil War articles, most notably *Military Affairs* and *Strategy & Tactics.*

Interest Groups

Civil War Round Tables exist in many cities. These regularly have discussions, lectures, trips, and other activities, and can be immensely useful for developing contacts and collecting unusual information. Civil War Round Table Associates (POB 7388, Little Rock, AK, 72217) is a central clearing house on the location of the many Round Tables.

Numerous reenactment groups are active, mostly in the United States, though several are in Britain and elsewhere. These regularly stage skirmishes in Civil War dress. Several such groups are particularly adept at recreating the minute technical details of military life and practice during the Civil War. The various Civil War journals regularly carry articles and ads dealing with reenactment groups.

Simulation Games

There are no simulation games which deal with the entire Chickamauga Campaign, though various aspects of it have been dealt with in varying degrees of accuracy and interest. The Battle of Chickamauga has been the subject of several simulation games. The most notable of these is West End's *Chickamauga: The Confederacy's Last Hope* (1986), designed by John Southard, which won the Charles Roberts' Award for the best pre-twentieth century wargame published in 1986. Other games of interest are *Chickamauga* [*Blue and Gray Quad*] (SPI, 1984), *Chickamauga: River of Death* (Phoenix, 1985), and *The Battle of Chickamauga* (Flying Buffalo, 1974). The struggle for Chattanooga is treated in *Chattanooga* [*Blue and Gray Quad II*] (SPI, 1975).